To access online media visit:
www.halleonard.com/mylibrary
1992-5013-0813-6026

PRODUCING MUSIC WITH PRO TOOLS 11

quick**PRO**
guides

PRODUCING MUSIC WITH PRO TOOLS 11

Glenn Lorbecki and Greg "Stryke" Chin

Hal Leonard Books
An Imprint of Hal Leonard Corporation

Published in 2014 by Hal Leonard Books
An Imprint of Hal Leonard Corporation
7777 West Bluemound Road
Milwaukee, WI 53213

Trade Book Division Editorial Offices
33 Plymouth St., Montclair, NJ 07042

Printed in the United States of America
Book design by Adam Fulrath
Book composition by Kristina Rolander and Bill Gibson

Library of Congress Cataloging-in-Publication Data

Lorbecki, Glenn.
 Producing music with Pro Tools 11 / Glenn Lorbecki and Greg "Stryke" Chin.
     pages cm
 Includes index.
 ISBN 978-1-4803-5508-8
 1. Pro Tools. 2. Digital audio editors. I. Stryke (Musician) II. Title.
 ML74.4.P76L674 2014
 781.3'4536--dc23
                          2014038007

www.halleonardbooks.com

CONTENTS

Chapter 2

Chapter 3

Chapter 4

Chapter 5

Chapter 6

Chapter 7

PREFACE

Welcome to *Producing Music with Pro Tools 11*! This latest version of Pro Tools builds on the solid platform established and refined by AVID/Digidesign over the last 20 years, and is used by the most successful and creative engineers in the business to create the music we love so well. Pro Tools has become the de facto standard for music production and audio post-production for visual media, and you will find it in virtually every major recording facility and project studio around the world. Because of this ubiquity, it is to the advantage of every serious engineer to learn this platform thoroughly in order to get the most from your sessions. Whether you're working at home or trading files with someone across the globe, Pro Tools is a complete production environment for recording, mixing, and mastering music at the highest professional standard of quality.

Before we get started, we should outline our goals: if your aim is to arm yourself with the tools you need to be more effective at mixing and mastering music, then we are in complete harmony. The goal of this book is to get you familiar with the concepts of producing music, including getting ready, using processors, tracking vocals and instruments, and getting it all to work together, all within the Pro Tools environment. These are complex tasks, and you will need to commit a fair amount of time to learn all the techniques required to become proficient. If you put in the effort—and use this book as a guide—you will be turning out music that sounds better than ever before.

ACKNOWLEDGMENTS

Writing a book is one of the things I never thought I'd actually get to accomplish in my life. My entire career has been devoted to music, and as I've gotten little older (but not necessarily wiser), I've had the opportunity to expand that career in so many ways. While I love writing and performing music as an artist, producer, and DJ, I also love speaking to audiences as a representative for Avid and others. Assisting in the writing of this book has been one of the highlights of my career. I would like to thank Glenn Lorbecki and Bill Gibson for asking me to be a part of this project. Your belief in me and your guidance has been absolutely essential! I'd also like to thank and acknowledge my fellow team members and friends at Avid, led by the incomparable Gil Gowing.

I have the honor of working alongside some of the best and sharpest minds in the industry. Thanks for all the knowledge you and the rest of the team have imparted to me during my time there. Thanks to you all! I hope you all enjoy reading and using this book as much as I have enjoyed working on it. —Greg

I must acknowledge those who make it possible for me to pursue my passion and to present in this book some of the experience and knowledge I've gained. Bill Gibson has stepped forward to give me the opportunity to write this book, and others, for Hal Leonard Books. Greg "Stryke" Chin has brought his intimate knowledge of the platform to this series, and I've enjoyed our collaboration!

To the many engineers, producers, musicians, and directors I've worked with over the years, I offer my humble thanks, as I've learned something from each and every one of you. You've given me tools for my toolbox and arrows for my quiver, targets to shoot for, and obstacles to avoid. We build on the knowledge and accomplishments of those who preceded us. It is my sincere hope that this book might provide some enlightenment and, perhaps, inspiration for the next wave of music makers.

I would like to acknowledge some other kind people for their assistance in this process: Kisha Kalahiki, James Nixon, and the great Bob Ludwig, with whom I co-chaired the Recording Academy Producers & Engineers Wing for five years.

Let's not forget Keely Whitney (www.KeelyWhitney.com) for the use of her wonderful music, the Mahavishnu Orchestra for the endless inspiration, and of course, AVID. —Glenn

INTRODUCTION

Welcome to *Producing Music with Pro Tools 11*! Whether you're a new engineer or a veteran of the decibel wars, this book can be a tool to help guide you through the process of recording music using Pro Tools, one of the most powerful DAW platforms in the world.

The latest version of Pro Tools builds on the solid platform established and refined by Digidesign/AVID since 1991 and is used by the top engineers in the business to create music in nearly every imaginable genre. Pro Tools has become the de facto standard for music production, audio post-production for visual media, and game audio production, and you will find it in virtually every major recording facility and project studio worldwide. Because of this ubiquity, it is to the advantage of every serious engineer to learn the platform thoroughly, in order to work efficiently and get the most from each session. Whether you're working at home or trading files with someone across the globe, Pro Tools is a complete production environment for recording music at the highest professional level of quality.

Let's take a moment to outline our goals: In order to get the most out of this book, you should be geared toward improving your engineering skills and experimenting with new production techniques. The goal of this book is to help you become familiar with the concepts of recording various instruments and vocals, what it takes to create a professional recording, how to edit (or "comp") your takes, and how to do all of this within the Pro Tools environment. These can be complex tasks, and you will need to commit a good deal of time to learn all the techniques required to become proficient. If you put in the effort—and use this book as a guide—you will be recording tracks that sound better than ever before.

Thank you for letting me be a part of your creative journey. I hope you enjoy the ride!

What Should You Bring to the Party?

In addition to having access to your own working Pro Tools rig, there are a few skills you'll need to take full advantage of the information presented to you in this book.

- **Computers:** You must possess an above average understanding of computers in order to make the most of your Pro Tools software and, indeed, of any professional DAW software system.
- **Engineering:** You should have a working knowledge of audio engineering concepts, signal flow, and gain structure and have an understanding of the language of audio production.
- **Music:** It helps to have a background in music. It may seem obvious to some folks, but there are terms and concepts in music production that we use constantly, and these terms are not always self-evident—such as *verse, chorus,* and *bridge;* or *tempo, crescendo,* and *intonation.* This is the language of music, and it's very handy for understanding and communicating ideas.
- **Music Theory:** It also helps to have had some music theory education, even if self-taught. A good producer can tell if a particular note or chord is working within a song and can make suggestions and fixes when it's not working. (This, of course, is subjective—never assume that a half-step harmony interval is a mistake.)
- **Patience:** Pro Tools is a very deep and complex program, and it can take years to fully understand all the features. I've been using Pro Tools for over a decade yet have learned many new things in the course of researching this book series. I will give you basic information on each subject initially, then delve into deeper levels of understanding and complexity. Get familiar with the basics, and practice your skills, so you can move on to the more difficult material with confidence.
- **Learn more than one way to do things**: This will come in handy in many situations, such as when you are editing audio and need to cut out a clip and drag it to another track. I can think of at least four different ways to do it, each with its own set of advantages, each depending on the page I'm on and the editing tool I have currently selected. Learn to be versatile, and practice with the tools often; through repetition you will become an expert.

How to Use This Book and Related Online Materials

This book is designed to quickly bring you up to speed on the power and capabilities of recording instruments and vocals with Pro Tools, and to make you a more competent and confident Pro Tools user overall. A good deal of this confidence will come from knowing that your system is properly installed and configured.

Some people are visual learners—that is, they need to see an image in order to get a firm grasp of abstract subjects. Throughout the book, you will see pictures or screen captures that illustrate the function or the process as described in the text. Use these to be sure you're viewing the same information or screen being covered on that page.

Not all information is applicable to both native/host-based and DSP-based systems. Where there is a difference, I will point out the distinction.

Since we'll be learning a lot of new key command shortcuts in each chapter, you will find a table of the keystrokes covered in each section of the book. All keystroke examples will be given in Mac user format. Here is a comparison table for basic Mac vs. Windows key equivalents to get started:

Mac OS X	Windows 7
Control Key (Ctrl)	Control Key (Ctrl)
Option Key (Opt)	Start Key (Win) also called Windows Key
Command Key (⌘, Apple)	Alt
Return Key	Enter Key, main keyboard only
Delete Key	Backspace Key

There will also be a brief self-exam at the conclusion of each chapter so you can brush up on germane material before moving on. Experienced Pro Tools users will find this to be a particularly useful exercise, as some of the Pro Tools operations may have been changed or modified from previous versions.

I will give you as many practical uses and examples as possible so that you can benefit from some shortcuts and a more streamlined work flow. Work with these exercises as much as you can; it will make the techniques seem like second nature.

Since most of the work you'll be doing is in stereo, we will assume that stereo is the default main output or destination format for examples given in the book.

Feel free to do what I do when reading a book like this: dog-ear the pages, take notes in the margins, use a highlighter, paste sticky notes on important pages, keep it next to your DAW—whatever it takes to make this info easily accessible so that you'll actually *use* it.

Terminology
There are some terms with which you may be unfamiliar or that are used in specific ways in this book. Take a moment to review definitions of these common terms in the glossary section at the back of the book.

Video Content
We have prepared a number of videos showing in detail some of the operations discussed in this book. You can watch the videos anytime just by downloading the online video files. This requires QuickTime or other video playback software for your Mac or PC.

Session Data and Audio Files
Also provided online are a number of Pro Tools sessions so that you'll have access to the audio and session setups for many of the exercises or operations described in the book. Just copy the session files to the local hard drive you have already set up for Pro Tools sessions. You may want to create a new directory named "Demo Exercises," just to be sure this data is kept separate from your other sessions. As you create or open these sessions, select Save As in the Pro Tools File menu and name the session using your initials as the first characters of the file name. This way you can easily locate your version of the exercises and still be able to open the original files if you should lose some data or need to start over.

In the event that you are unable to read or import session data, you can import audio files into a new session by pressing Shift + Command + I and selecting the files to be imported. When asked, create a new track for each file, and align it to the sequence start time. Using this method, you will have to import (or re-create) the other session settings, but the audio files should all be in sync.

Additional Materials

We have dedicated a section of our website to provide you with easy access to downloads of important files to aid you in your productions. These include pre-production planning worksheets, input lists, tracking sheets, a list of common Pro Tools error codes, and even a handy key command roadmap to help you work faster and more efficiently.

Here's the link: www.GlennSound.com/PT

Drop me a line, let me know if this is helpful information, or suggest what other information you would find useful. Ping me: PT@GlennSound.com

Updates

Occasionally some information will be updated to reflect new software releases or revisions. Check my website from time to time to see what's new in the world of Pro Tools as it relates to this book. You will also find a list of selected links to support websites, manufacturers, and other resources that will help you in your pursuit of audio excellence.

Summary of Key Commands

Operation	Key Command
Import Audio Files	Shift + Command + 1

Chapter 1
Pro Tools Primer

First order of business: your Pro Tools system needs to be running properly before working on any of the recording techniques in this book. If you already have Pro Tools 11 installed and your hardware is operating properly, then you're ready to rock and can skip past the "What's New" section of the book, going directly to chapter 2. If you are using version 9 or earlier, you should read the next section carefully, as it will give you a quick overview of what to expect from newer versions of Pro Tools.

It is very important that you follow all of the instructions in the Pro Tools software and hardware installation guides that come with your Pro Tools system purchase. This book can help guide you through system settings and configuration, but the installation of your particular software modules and hardware I/O is unique to you, so you should always refer to the "Getting Started" guides and "Read Me" files in order to get your Digital Audio Workstation (DAW) up and running. Once you have the basic system operating properly, use this book as a guide to fine-tune system performance and get the most out of your Pro Tools configuration.

If you encounter problems with the initial installation of your software or hardware, you should visit (and bookmark) the section of the AVID audio forums website dedicated to addressing up-to-the-minute changes and "known issues." This is referred to as the Digi User Conference, or DUC; the website URL is http://duc.avid.com/

It can be frustrating to encounter computer problems while trying to get up to speed on new software. While Pro Tools is equally stable on both OS X and Windows 7 and 8 platforms, you still need to have a machine with sufficient RAM, disk space, and data I/O ports. It's important to check your computer's specifications to be sure they are compatible with the current release of Pro Tools software. See the "Studio Basics" chapter of this book to determine if your computer is compatible and capable of running the software according to AVID specs. There is also a list of supported OS versions maintained on the AVID website: http://avid.force.com/pkb/articles/en_US /compatibility/Pro-Tools-11-System-Requirements?NewLang=en&DocType=1083& popup=true&q=pro+tools+compatibility&y=0&x=0

What's New in Pro Tools 11?

Since the last major upgrade to Pro Tools, the folks at Avid have been working on an upgrade that revolutionizes the way we look at buying audio workstation software and hardware. The upgrades are numerous, and we can't possibly cover them all in the scope of this book, but we will certainly delve into the changes that deal directly with mixing and mastering. Let's take a look at what's new . . .

Digidesign Is Now AVID

AVID has owned Digi since 1995, and 2010 marked the emergence of AVID as the sole brand identity for all their audio and video software and hardware lines. As a result, the Digidesign brand name has been phased out. However, the Pro Tools name lives on, as does its reputation for being the industry standard for professional audio production. Now let's take a brief look at some of the new features of AVID's Pro Tools 11 that will have an impact on the way we work.

Drag and Drop Installation

Installation of the Pro Tools software is much simpler with the drag and drop software installer.

64-Bit Architecture

Pro Tools 11 software code has been rewritten from the ground up as a 64-bit program, which means increased memory space, support for huge, complex sessions, and support for RAM-intensive virtual instruments.

AAX Plug-in Support

AVID's new hybrid AAX plug-in format operates in both HDX accelerated DSP mode and Native mode. This replaces the older HDTDM and RTAS plug-in formats, which will no longer be supported.

DAE Is Dead, Long Live AAE

The Digidesign Audio Engine (DAE) has been replaced by the AVID Audio Engine (AAE), allowing you to unleash the power of your host computer for processing audio. Users will see dramatic performance improvements whether using HDX or Native processing. The new AAE supports dynamic plug-in processing, whereby your system allocates system resources only when an audio program is present, thereby preserving precious processing power and increasing plug-in counts systemwide.

Aggregate I/O

This is where all of your I/O hardware comes together to create the ultimate in system flexibility. You will be able to hook up your audio interfaces all at once. The new Pro Tools audio engine allows you to connect and select from your list of I/O options, in many cases without having to restart Pro Tools.

Dual Audio Buffers

Pro Tools uses a low-latency buffer for record and input channels, and a fixed high buffer size for playback tracks. This allows Native system users to record new session tracks with minimum delay, even while playing back existing tracks.

Offline Bounce

Finally—you can bounce mixes using faster-than-real-time mix delivery. This is huge. You can also create multiple mixes simultaneously using faster-than-real-time bounce.

Gobbler users—with a mouse click, you can upload audio mixes to the cloud in Pro Tools.

Advanced Metering

Tired of viewing peak meters? Pro Tools 11 now offers 17 different professional-standard scale and ballistic settings for your session metering needs (HD version). Inserts show mini level meters for each plug-in, and gain-reduction metering appears beside regular meters on channels using dynamics plug-ins. Output meters are now visible in the toolbar.

Avid Video Engine

A newly redesigned video engine uses the same core engine as Media Composer. You can now play back AVID DNXHD video in Pro Tools output to AVID, AJA, or Blackmagic Peripherals.

Insert Bypass Shortcuts

Using a few key-command shortcuts, you can now quickly enable/disable some or all plug-in inserts. These can be activated by insert row (A–E, F–J) or by type (EQ, Dynamics, Reverb, Delay, Modulation).

New Automation Features

Power users have been asking for this for a long time; now Pro Tools 11 can write automation data in real-time during recording. Automation data will now be time-stamped, so automation data will be preserved when moving clips.

New Workspace Browser

A new 64-bit database engine enables ultra-fast file searching. Now you can use a unified session and workspace browser to quickly locate your data files.

Satellite Technology

Satellite Mode, the ability to link multiple Pro Tools 11 systems, is now standard in HD11. Link up to 12 HD systems with a simple Ethernet connection. Is video playback slowing you down? Use a second computer to play video files using Video Satellite LE with Pro Tools 11. Video Satellite is now compatible with Media Composer 7.

GUI Improvements

Along with improved display performance, AVID has refined the look and feel of the user interface.

Session Import/Export

Now all Pro Tools users will be able to import and export OMF and AAF formatted files without having to purchase or install additional software. This is great news for Pro Tools operators who regularly exchange files with users of other DAW systems. There are advanced Import Session Data options, which were formerly only available with Pro Tools HDX systems. You now have the ability to bounce MP3 files to disk, which formerly required purchase of the MP3 Export option.

We will examine some of these new features in detail as we get into the various chapters in this book. There will be examples of how to maximize your system performance, activate and access your I/O, and make the most of the production techniques available with these new and expanded tools. It's good to know that all of your Pro Tools skills will now translate equally between the different levels of software. This is an amazingly versatile software platform; learning how to navigate through the program and use all of its features will make you a better engineer, and as a result, your music will sound better too.

Software Overview

Even the basic version of Pro Tools incorporates some of the features and functionality of Pro Tools HD:

- Automatic Delay Compensation is perhaps the biggest benefit of moving up to Pro Tools. Every version of Pro Tools now offers ADC, which allows you much more flexibility in selecting and applying plug-ins and saves tons of time in having to manually calculate latency.
- Use *any* ASIO or Core Audio–compliant audio interface.
- I/O settings have changed; busses now include output busses as well as internal-mix busses. Output busses can overlap, facilitating sharing of physical outputs. I/O settings can be imported or ignored on opening a session.
- DigiBase search and catalog functions have been enhanced.
- Import and export OMF/AAF sequences.

Hardware Overview: Two Levels of Performance

Pro Tools provides a single software solution for all supported AVID hardware, and now, Pro Tools offers support for third-party audio interfaces that utilize compatible Core Audio and/or ASIO drivers. If you're a longtime user of Pro Tools, this will be a revolutionary change in the right direction. With your iLok attached, Pro Tools will even run your session without *any* hardware interface attached. This is another major change in Pro Tools 9 and higher.

Your Pro Tools performance will be determined by the mode you have installed on your iLok device:

Level 1: Pro Tools

- This is the standard software mode for Pro Tools when a non-HD audio engine is selected.
- Requires a Pro Tools iLok authorization.

Features

- Up to 32 channels of I/O.
- Up to 96 audio tracks (depending on sample rate).
- Up to 128 instrument tracks.
- 512 MIDI tracks.
- 128 aux tracks.
- 256 busses.
- 1 video track.

Hardware Requirements

- Can be used with any supported AVID interface on Mac or PC. (Pro Tools does *not* support the 001 family or the first-generation Mbox.) See the website for revised listings: http://avid.force.com/pkb/articles/en_US/compatibility/Pro-Tools-11 -Approved-Audio-Interfaces-and-Peripherals
- Any ASIO or Core Audio–supported I/O should be recognized by the system.
- A number of audio-interface manufacturers are now touting their Pro Tools compatibility, including Apogee, MOTU, Presonus, and others. Check your local pro audio dealer, or consult the Interwebs for more info.
- See the section on Aggregate I/O for more info on how to access your interface(s) within Pro Tools.

Connection

Depending on your audio interface, any USB or FireWire port on the computer itself should work like a charm. Ports attached to USB keyboards typically do not have enough current to power hard drives or interfaces. Check the AVID website to find out if your legacy Digidesign I/O device is supported.

Calibration

Each manufacturer has its own calibration or setup protocol, depending on which I/O you choose. See the later section on system calibration for more details on DIY calibration methods.

Plug-ins

Pro Tools comes with an extensive bundle of plug-ins and virtual instruments designed to get you up and running right away.

See the website for details: www.avid.com/US/products/Pro-Tools-Software /Specifications

Level 2: Pro Tools HD

- Pro Tools runs in this mode when you connect supported HD or HD Native hardware and have selected the appropriate interface in your audio engine settings.
- Requires a valid Pro Tools HD iLok authorization.

Features

As of this writing, the Mac spec for running Pro Tools software is as follows:

- Up to 192 channels of I/O
- Up to 768 audio tracks (depending on sample rate)
- 256 instrument tracks
- 512 MIDI tracks
- 512 aux tracks
- 256 busses
- 64 video tracks
- HDX systems take on the heavy lifting part of DSP using a dedicated 64-bit floating point mix bus

Hardware

- Use either Pro Tools HD Native or Pro Tools HD interfaces. HD also requires HDX PCIe DSP Acceleration cards. HD Native requires either a PCIe Core card or an HD Native Thunderbolt interface.
- An HD Native Core card gives you up to 64 I/O channels and 256 tracks using host processing (no DSP).
- HD Native can be used with the HD OMNI, HD I/O, and HD MADI interfaces. Each HDX card offers 256 voices and can support up to four HD series audio interfaces.

Connection

- A multi-pair cable connects the PCIe card to the outboard audio interface(s).
- If you plan to use a computer, such as a Mac Mini, or a laptop that does not support PCIe cards, you will need an expansion chassis, a PCIe controller card, and a cable to connect to the PCIe controller card in your computer. (The expansion chassis includes card and cable.)

Calibration

- The HD I/O interfaces offer access to rear panel calibration pots. See the later section on calibration for details.

Plug-ins

Pro Tools HD runs the AAX 64-bit plug-in format. See the AVID website for more info and up-to-date availability.

Outboard Gear

The really cool part about working with outboard gear in Pro Tools is the ability of the system to calculate and compensate for delays introduced by using outboard signal-processing devices in a send/return configuration. In other words, you can take analog audio from any interface, send it to an outboard compressor (for example), return the compressed audio to the interface, and let Pro Tools calculate the round-trip delay. You can then set the system to compensate for that delay systemwide. This is a great solution for digital/analog hybrid-system users.

Refer to the section on hardware inserts for instructions on how to connect your outboard gear.

iLok

Pro Tools copy-protection authorizations reside on an iLok USB dongle, which comes with your Pro Tools software. Most plug-in manufacturers now authorize their software via iLok as well.

- **The Pluses:** Portable, safe, convenient, reliable. A great way to store all of your authorizations in one place and easily transport them from studio to studio or machine to machine.
- **The Minuses:** An iLok is small and can be lost or broken if you're not careful. Replacing authorizations can be very costly, unless you buy "Zero down-time" license protection.

System Calibration

To be certain your hardware and software are passing audio properly, you should devise a regular regimen for calibrating your system. Since audio equipment operates best within its own range of input/output voltages, it's a good idea to set up each piece of gear so that it can connect to the next piece of gear in line and still be within its comfortable operating voltage range.

The basic principle is to apply a fixed-level input signal to a hardware input, then adjust each gain stage in the system to maintain optimal operating level. This level is typically 0 dBVU (-14 dBFS).

Some audio I/O hardware may have physical input and output calibration accessible via trim pots. See the owner's manual for exact calibration instructions for your interface.

Pro Tools HD I/O Calibration Mode

Pro Tools HD I/O users can use Calibration mode to help adjust input and output levels. There are detailed instructions here included in the manual, but the shorthand version looks like this:

1. Connect a Pro Tools output to a VU meter on a console or other recording device.
2. Use a Signal Generator plug-in on a channel to send a 1 kHz tone through an output channel to the meter.
3. Adjust level via the Output Trim pot on the back of the I/O unit until the VU meter reads 0 dB. Repeat these steps for each physical output channel.
4. Connect all of the I/O device outputs directly to the I/O inputs.
5. Route the Signal Generator track output to *all* outputs.
6. Select Calibration mode from the Options menu. All track names will flash, and small arrows at the bottom of each track will point up or down to indicate whether you need to adjust the Input Trim pot up or down to achieve the level you've selected in the calibration-level Preferences menu.
7. Adjust the I/O Input Trim pot accordingly. When you've trimmed to the exact level on a track, that track name will stop flashing.

Modify the levels in this procedure to match your configuration.

Optimizing the Pro Tools Environment

Tweaking Pro Tools for recording and overdubbing is a little different than for mixing. You will need to adjust some of the system settings to fine-tune your computer for the recording process. It's fairly simple, and you can use this section as a guide to walk you through the steps in getting the most out your Pro Tools rig.

System Usage Window

Having this window open on your desktop will keep you informed as to the performance of your Pro Tools session by displaying system status in real-time. On non-HD systems, you will see three meters in the Activity window:

- **CPU:** Shows current computer CPU usage as a percentage of the allocated processing capacity.
- **Disk:** Displays the amount of activity on the disk bus or busses as a percentage of total capacity.
- **Memory:** Shows how much RAM is being used by Pro Tools.

For HD|HDX Systems

The System Usage window displays the CPU, disk use, and memory as above, but you will see a few other windows as well, depending on the cards installed on your system.

- **Disk Cache:** Shows the percentage of the allocated memory being used to cache audio in the session.
- **Voices:** Shows how many voices of your total voice allocation are being used.
- **Time Slots:** Shows how many time slots of your total allocation are being used.

Playback Engine

Whether you are using Pro Tools or Pro Tools HD software, you will need to adjust the parameters for host-based operation. This is referred to as Optimizing Host-Based Pro Tools Performance. HD Native and standard Pro Tools users rely on host-based processing for recording, playback, mixing, and real-time effects processing. Even if you are using HDX cards, the computer host still handles the chore of real-time effects processing.

- First, access the Playback Engine menu by choosing Setup > Playback Engine…Your current engine will be displayed in the drop-down menu at the top of the Playback Engine window.

```
Playback Engine

Playback Engine:  Pro Tools Aggregate I/O  ▼

Settings
           H/W Buffer Size:  256 Samples       ▼
              Host Engine:  ☐ Ignore Errors During Playback/Record
                               (may cause clicks and pops)
                           ☑ Dynamic Plug-in Processing
             Video Engine:  ☐ Enable

Disk Playback
     Cache Size:  Normal                ▼
     Lower values for the disk buffer reduce memory usage.  Higher values improve disk performance.

                                              [ OK ]
```

- This menu will display a list of available connected I/O devices. Select your preferred device from the list. If you are selecting Pro Tools Aggregate I/O or any hardware other than the current device, Pro Tools will ask you to quit and restart in order to make that device active.

Buffer Settings

When recording, you should use the minimum buffer settings. This will allow you to do faster audio processing and keep audio latency (delay) to a minimum. Locate the H/W Buffer Size menu, then select the lowest setting available for your system.

Host Engine

This check-box option asks if you would like to ignore errors during playback or record. The next statement says it all– "may cause clicks and pops." Ignore this command entirely and leave the box unchecked, unless you are having issues with record or playback errors. Should you decide to check it, you'll get an additional check box which, if checked, says it will "Minimize Additional I/O Latency." Again, this is not recommended, unless you are having record or playback errors.

Delay Compensation Engine

This setting is no longer a part of the Playback Engine settings. If turned on, ADC will automatically be set to the highest delay limit (16,838 samples). Select Options > Delay Compensation to toggle the on/off state.

Dynamic Plug-in Processing

This check-box option, if checked, will allow Pro Tools to only use CPU power on plug-ins when they are actually processing audio. Therefore, if they aren't doing anything, no additional system power will be used. This can be very handy if you have a large number of plug-ins in your session.

Video Engine

This checkbox can be left unchecked if your session has no video in it. Since Pro Tools 11 has a brand new audio engine, the video engine is now seperate from the audio engine. It's actually built on Avid's Media Composer engine. Having these engines seperate, contributes to even more efficient use of resources in Pro Tools. Of course, if you will be working with video, make sure to have this box checked.

Cache Size

This relates to Elastic Audio processing and the RAM that AAE allocates for pre-buffering audio. The standard setting is Normal, though you may need to raise the cache size if you encounter Elastic Audio errors, or lower it to free up memory for other system performance requirements.

Apply Changes

When you have made all applicable changes to your Playback Engine, click OK to exit. Again, if you have made changes to your Hardware I/O Engine, you will have to quit and restart Pro Tools.

Very Important Note!

If you start Pro Tools without the previously selected Hardware I/O connected and powered up, Pro Tools *will not* launch! Instead, it will go part way through the boot process, then pause to display an error message that reads: "Pro Tools could not initiate the current playback device. Please make sure that the device has been configured correctly."

Don't worry; just click OK, then relaunch Pro Tools while holding down the "N" key. This will bring up the Playback Engine dialog, which will allow you to select another interface or use the computer's built-in I/O. Click OK, and you're off and running. In fact, if you like, you can use the hardware I/O modifier key command to call up the Playback Engine dialog every time you launch Pro Tools.

PC users should make sure the ASIO drivers are installed before using Pro Tools.

Hardware Settings

- The Pro Tools Hardware Setup menu gives you the option to set word clock source, sample rate, and digital I/O for your hardware, depending on the type of audio interface you have connected to your computer.
- Any device that is supported by Core Audio drivers (Mac) or ASIO drivers (PC) can be configured in this menu, including your computer's built-in sound options via Pro Tools Aggregate I/O.
- Choose Setup > Hardware to access the Hardware Setup window.

Peripherals

This window identifies the connected I/O device or allows you to select the device to be configured if you have multiple I/O devices connected.

Sample Rate

- If no session is open, you can use this window to select the default sample rate for Pro Tools operation. This would apply to new sessions as you create them.
- Note: you can also specify a sample rate in the dialog window when creating a new session.
- In opening an existing session, Pro Tools would assume the sample rate at which that session was created. In which case, the Sample Rate option would not be available for modification.

Clock Source

- This drop-down menu lets you select the digital clock source Pro Tools will use as a reference.
- Select Internal if recording analog audio, unless you have an external clock source connected.
- The S/PDIF (RCA) setting is for use when recording from the S/PDIF RCA digital input, and will synchronize Pro Tools to the output of the external digital device.
- Use the Optical setting when recording from an optical digital source. You will have to select Format from the following menu in order to match the source signal.

Optical Format

- **ADAT:** Choose this setting from the drop-down menu if your source is emitting ADAT Optical digital multi-channel output (Lightpipe) connected via fiber-optic cable. Supports session sample rates up to 48 kHz only.
- **S/PDIF:** This refers to optical two-channel S/PDIF digital signal input via optical TOSLINK cable only.

Launch Setup App

Use this command when setting up your third-party I/O device. This will launch the control panel specifically designed for your audio interface.

Disk Allocation

This menu refers to the location of the folder from which your audio will be played back—per track.

Suggestion: If your session is displaying audio waveforms and playing back audio correctly, *do not change these settings.*

I/O Settings

Choose Setup > I/O to access the I/O settings for your specific audio interface. From this window, you can select the following:

- **Input:** Here you can name any input channel, per input, per device. You may also turn any input on/off, change routing, or add new input paths to your configuration.
- **Output:** This menu is where you name output channels, activate or deactivate output paths, change routing, or add new output paths. You may assign an Audition Path for Audio Suite previews, Clip List auditions, and so forth. You may also assign a destination for the solo bus, if you choose to send it somewhere other than the main outputs.

- **Bus:** There are major changes in bus assignments beginning with Pro Tools 9. Whereas you used to see all available busses in this tab, now you only need to see the ones you create for your session.

In fact, that's a good place to start. Let's set up a sample bus page for monitor outputs:

Step 1: Open the I/O > Bus tab and delete all bus paths. Yes, you read correctly, *delete all bus paths*. Now you can create a new, clean routing page with only the info you need for your session.

Step 2: Click on the New Path button. In the pop-up dialog, create one new Stereo path, name it "Monitor Out," then click OK. The new path will appear in the Bus window.

Step 3: Tick the box next to the Mapping to Output window; this will create a link between the Monitor Output path you created and the I/O hardware output pair A 1–2. The Monitor Out bus will now become the main output assignment for all of the tracks in your session.

Step 4: You can create new busses in this window, or you can use the "new track…" command from the Send pane of the Edit or Mix windows to create a new Aux Input path as required for your session. Find that menu by clicking on the Send button, then click "new track…"

Step 5: To make a reverb send, create a Stereo Aux Input, sample based, and name it "Reverb"; tick the box marked "Create next to current track"; then click Create. In one simple operation, you have created a reverb send/return path with all assignments readymade.

Repeat these steps as necessary to create new destinations for your session.

Note: This send/return operation is also described in the send section of this book.

Handy Pro Tools Functions

There are a number of edit modes and edit tools for manipulating sequence elements in Pro Tools.

Edit Modes

Shuffle (F1)

Shuffle mode allows you to move clips without leaving gaps or to insert new clips between adjacent clips while forcing subsequent clips downstream. This is also known as a *ripple edit*. Trimming a clip in Shuffle mode will affect the timing of all clips downstream. (This does not apply to MIDI notes).

Slip (F2)

As the name suggests, this mode allows you to move or *slip* clips in time or between tracks. Slip is the default mode for editing operations.

Spot (F3)

Clicking on a clip in Spot mode brings up a dialog box that enables you to type in a precise time code or bar/beat location point. This is particularly handy if you've accidentally moved a clip from its original recording time and need to get it back to where it once belonged.

Grid (F4)

Allows you to snap clips and MIDI notes to precise time increments, whether minutes/seconds, feet/frames, or bars/beats. Moving a note or clip using Absolute Grid snaps the start exactly to the nearest time increment on the grid, even if it was initially between beats or other grid markings.

Relative Grid aligns the note or clip to the grid relative to its initial starting position. For example, if clip A is between beats 1 and 2 of the bar, it will be moved left or right in quarter-note increments, but will retain its original timing between beats.

Edit Tools

Zoomer Tool

The Zoomer tool zooms in and out on the timeline. In Normal Zoom mode, the Zoomer tool remains selected even after the zooming. Single Zoom mode allows you to use Zoom once; the tool then reverts to its previously selected non-zooming tool.

Trim Tool

Shortens or extends the duration of a clip or MIDI note by clicking and dragging the start or end of the clip.

Selector Tool

Selects an area within a clip or track for editing or playback.

Grabber Tool

The Grabber tool enables you to select an entire clip and move it within the track or to other tracks within the timeline.

Scrubber Tool

Drag the Scrubber tool across audio tracks in the Edit window to locate an edit point or hear a particular section within an audio clip. We used to "scrub" tape back and forth over the playback head on a reel-to-reel tape recorder to find a musical downbeat for editing or cuing.

Pencil Tool

- Used for re-drawing waveforms to eliminate a click or pop in an audio file. Must be zoomed in to the sample view level in order to activate.
- May be used for drawing in MIDI notes.
- May also be used for drawing automation breakpoints.
- Can draw various shapes for automating pan, volume, and other parameters.
- Shapes include line, triangle, square, random, and freehand.

Smart Tool

Click on this gem to have immediate access to the Selector, Grabber, and Trim tools, depending on where the cursor hovers over a track, clip, or automation lane. The Smart tool also performs single-click fades and cross-fades.

Modifier Keys

The modifier keys are the Shift, Control, Option, and Command keys. (On a PC, those keys are Shift, Control, Windows, and Alt.) Pro Tools allows you to modify keystrokes and mouse-clicks depending on the modifier key. In some cases, various combinations of modifier keys will be used to achieve different results. For example, while Command + Click (Alt + Click on PC) brings up a tool menu for the cursor, Control + Command + Click (Control + Alt + Click in Windows) performs a variety of functions depending on the menu clicked.

See a list of topic-specific key commands at the end of each chapter.

These Are a Few of My Favorite Tools

I leave the cursor tools set on Smart Tools all the time, except when I need a job-specific tool, such as TC/E or Pencil tool. Of the three choices for tools, I use the Trim tool, the Selector tool, and the Separation Grabber. These allow me to trim the beginning and end of a clip, highlight an area within a clip, and move clips or notes. The addition of the Separation Grabber allows me to highlight areas for deletion, copying, or moving, without disturbing the original clip or having to change to another tool.

You can easily change edit tools by pressing Command + Click and selecting from the pop-up menu, or by toggling through options by using function keys F5–F10.

Pro Tools Conventions

In order to navigate properly and actually locate the functions we will be exploring, you should understand a few of the terms we will be using to describe the screen landscape and layout in the Pro Tools environment.

- **Window:** This refers to a main display component, such as the Edit or Mix window or a plug-in window.
- **Pane:** This refers to a subset of an open window. An example would be the Tracks pane of the Edit window.
- **Button:** This would be any clickable graphic button that enables/disables functions or gives you access to a sub-menu. Clicking on the OK or Create button at the bottom of a pop-up window, for example.
- **Drop-Down Menu:** Any menu that opens to display more options when clicked is referred to as a drop-down menu. The Window menu at the top of the Pro Tools menu bar is a drop-down menu.
- **Pop-Up Window/Menu:** This could be a menu of functions or a new window that opens to display controls. Clicking on an assigned insert or send button displays a pop-up window.
- **Dialog Box:** This refers to any box that requires text input: naming a track, send, session name, or bounce file.

Key Commands

Most of the common operations in Pro Tools can be activated by a mouse-click or a keystroke. If you have a two-button mouse, there is a whole list of shortcuts available to you by performing a right-click on a menu or pane. There are nearly 30 pages of key command shortcuts in Pro Tools. Far too many to list here, but I will include the most-used commands as they pertain to each topic of the book. Memorizing these commands will save you lots of time and many miles of mousing.

There are custom keyboards, keyboard overlays, and stickers available from AVID and other third-party suppliers, such as Best Keyboard Stickers. If you work in Pro Tools a lot, it may be worth your while to look into those options to improve your work flow and speed up your process.

Keyboard Focus

The Pro Tools Keyboard Focus determines how the alpha keys function on your keyboard. There are three modes of operation, which will allow you to directly select clips in the clip list, enable or disable groups in the group list, or perform an edit or playback command. Only one Keyboard Focus mode can be active at a time—which disables the other two temporarily. Here are the different modes:

Commands Keyboard Focus

Selected in the Tracks pane of the Edit window. This enables a wide variety of single-key editing and playback commands accessible from the Edit window.

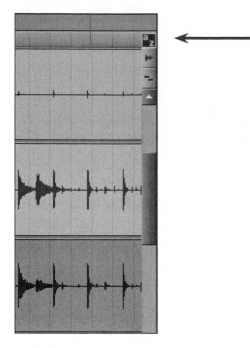

Note: Even if Commands Keyboard Focus mode is disabled, you can still access the command by using Control + the usual key.

Clip List Keyboard Focus

Selected in the upper-right corner of the Clips pane.

When enabled, you will be able to select audio and MIDI clips by typing the first few letters of the name.

Group List Keyboard Focus
Selected in the upper-right corner of the Groups pane.

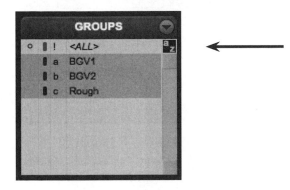

When enabled, you will be able to enable or disable groups by typing the Group ID letter that corresponds with the desired group.

Keyboard Focus access
Either click the a—z button in the panes as described, or type one of the following key commands:

Operation	Key Command
Cursor Tool Menu	Command + Click
Command Keyboard Focus	Command + Option + 1
Clip Keyboard Focus	Command + Option + 2
Groups Keyboard Focus	Command + Option + 3

Chapter 1 Review

1. With the introduction of _____, Pro Tools is now a ___-bit application.
2. Automatic _____compensation and third-party _____ support are now part of Pro Tools software.
3. Pro Tools requires the installation of a USB _____in order to authorize the system for operation of Pro Tools.
4. Pro Tools HD features near-zero latency record _____with AVID _____audio interfaces.
5. In order to run both AAX Native and _____ plug-ins, you will need to have an iLok authorized for Pro Tools HD, at least one _____ card installed in your computer, and an AVID interface designed for _____ operation.
6. The System _____ window tells you at a glance what percentage of _____ power you are using.
7. The Playback Engine dialog is used to fine-tune _____ performance.
8. _____ Hardware Buffer settings will result in greater latency but are preferable during mixing to allocate more power to effects processing and _____ plug-ins.
9. Starting Pro Tools software holding the ____ key will bring up the Playback Engine dialog, enabling you to designate a specific _____ device.
10. The Hardware Settings > Clock Source menu lets you select the session clock reference, whether _____ or _____.

11. Pro Tools has two optical input settings, _____ and _____ Lightpipe.

12. You configure all input and output assignments using the _____ menu.

13. The four main Edit modes in Pro Tools are _____, _____, _____, and _____ mode.

14. The main Edit tools are the _____ tool, _____ tool, _____ tool, _____ tool, _____ tool, and _____ tool.

15. The tool that performs multiple functions depending on the position within the track is called the _____ tool.

16. Pro Tools usually has several ways to complete an editing function. In addition to _____ commands, you can use numerous _____ shortcuts to complete tasks.

Chapter 2

BUILDING AND MANAGING YOUR VIRTUAL STUDIO

Just about every recording session is configured differently, so it can be a good idea to create your own sessions with custom settings that match your exact needs. These can be simple or complex, but it's worth your time to explore the options.

Session templates are a good place to start exploring Pro Tools capabilities and flexibility. Templates can help you understand how to create sessions and handle routing within Pro Tools. Open one of the music session templates to see examples of track layout, plug-in configuration, use of aux busses, and creation of a headphone mix.

Once you're familiar with these layouts, you can easily customize your own Pro Tools mixer to fit your tracking project. You can even create your own templates to use for your next tracking session.

Accessing Pro Tools Menus

Edit Window Menus

There are 12 main Edit Window menus, which give you access to configure the vast majority of available Pro Tools functions. Refer to this list when following menu selection instructions.

- **Pro Tools**: This menu gives you access to "About Pro Tools" version info and Preferences, and allows you to quit the program.
- **File**: Open sessions, create new sessions, save versions, bounce audio and video, import/export options, general info.
- **Edit**: Undo, cut/copy/paste options, clip editing commands.
- **View**: Display options.
- **Track**: Create and manage audio and MIDI tracks, manage track automation data.
- **Clip**: Manage audio and MIDI clips, including clip groups, looping, sync points, quantizing, and Elastic Audio properties.
- **Event**: Manage Time, Tempo, and Key operations for audio and MIDI tracks; activate Beat Detective.

- **Audio Suite**: Access to all Audio Suite functions for processing audio clips.
- **Options**: Manage record modes, transport control, and many other functional options for Pro Tools operation.
- **Setup**: Optimize system configurations, hardware routing, and access preferences.
- **Window**: Show, hide, and memorize screen display and window configurations.
- **Help**: Online and offline help is available on a variety of topics.

Configuring a Virtual Mixer in Pro Tools

Building a custom mixer in Pro Tools allows you to completely sidestep the pitfalls of traditional analog or physical digital consoles. Pro Tools mixers are limited only by the capacity of your particular system and I/O hardware.

If you grew up on analog recording consoles, you got used to the fact that there were *always* limitations. Either there weren't enough inputs, or you had to sub-mix channels in order to get sufficient outputs, or there were not enough sends; you get the idea. One of the first reasons to fall in love with Pro Tools is the ability to create *exactly* the right console you need to work on each and every song. Since the modules are virtual, you can grow or shrink the console to meet the immediate needs of your project.

Tracks

Each recorded audio channel should have its own track, as should aux returns, sub-masters, MIDI tracks, and virtual instruments. This way you can balance, monitor, and meter each instrument independently of the other audio tracks.

Stereo Pan Depth

Pro Tools now lets you select the amount of attenuation applied to signals panned to the center in a stereo mix. To access this setting from the Session Setup window, choose Setup > Session (Command + 2 on the numeric keypad). Select the Format tab, then click on the Pan Depth drop-down menu. You can choose from four different levels of attenuation:

- **-2.5 dB:** This is the only available setting for Pro Tools versions 8.x and below.
- **-3 dB:** This is the standard for many mixing consoles and is the default setting for Pro Tools 8.1 and above.
- **-4.5dB:** This is the standard center attenuation setting for SSL analog consoles.
- **-6 dB:** This is the standard for complete mono compatibility. Some US-made analog consoles offer the option of -3 dB or -6 dB center pan attenuation.

Changing these settings will result in a subtle change in the way sounds are perceived when panning across the center. A greater degree of pan attenuation will result in more subtle level-changes as signal is panned from side to side. Experiment to see if your mixes translate differently using the various settings.

Groups

When using several microphones to record an instrument, you can combine their tracks into groups, allowing you to control level, volume, pan, mute, solo, and record-enable, and edit functions of each member track with a single command.

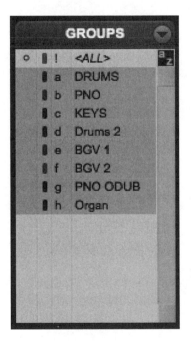

When recording a piano in stereo, for example, you would record each microphone onto its own mono track (instead of a single stereo track). This allows you to adjust level, and pan, mute, and solo independently of the other track. You can still group the two tracks to enable joint editing capabilities. Recording drums would be another example of an opportunity to use groups during a tracking session. Each group can have its own attributes or follow global edit commands. Grouped tracks maintain their own independent output assignments.

Sub-Masters

Sub-masters differ from groups, in that tracks feeding sub-masters can retain their parameter control independent of a group. Tracks feeding a sub-master are summed together into an auxiliary bus, the output of which is fed to the main output Master Mix bus.

Aux Sends/Returns

An Aux send is a parallel output from a track or tracks, which can be used to feed a sub-master (as above) or provide input to an effect device/plug-in. An aux has a level control, which can send signal *pre-fader* (independent of track volume control) or *post-fader* (subject to track volume control).

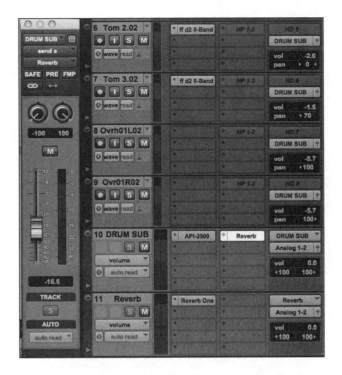

Pre-fader sends are used for headphone mixes, where you usually don't want the volume of individual tracks changing in the headphones while you adjust or solo tracks in your control-room mix. Another use for a pre-fader send would be to maintain a constant level of effect send on a track regardless of the track volume. An example of this would be setting up a chromatic tuner plug-in for monitoring guitar tuning. If using AAX Native plug-ins, those plugs will not remain active when record-enabled.

Post-fader sends are used for reverb, delay, and other effect sends where you would like the send level to follow the track volume control. Example: if you turn down the level of a vocal in a mix, you may want the reverb send level to get quieter in relation. You will find that your effects sound more balanced and natural when the send level scales up and down in relation to the track level.

Inserts

Pro Tools gives you ten inserts per track in two banks of five each:
A–E and F–J. These can either be software plug-in inserts, hardware inserts, or instrument plug-ins. With plug-ins and hardware inserts, the track signal is routed through your effect, then returned to the fader input on the same track. Inserts are pre-fader on audio, auxiliary, and instrument tracks; inserts are post-fader on Master Faders.

You can bypass inserts by Command + Clicking on the Insert button on a track in the Edit and Mix windows, or by clicking the Bypass button on the plug-in window itself.

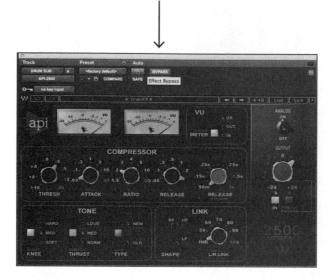

Repeat the command to toggle the in/out state.

Note: You can bypass the plug-ins in the "A" slot of every track by Option + Clicking on the Bypass button in any "A" slot plug-in window.

Likewise for plug-ins in the "B" slots, "C" slots, and so on. Repeat the command to toggle the bypass state.

Making an insert inactive will save system resources and voices. You can make an insert inactive by pressing Control + Command + Click on the Insert button. Repeat to toggle state.

Note: You can make all of the "A" slot plug-ins inactive by pressing Control + Option + Command + Click on a pane. (The "A" slot insert Control + Option + Command key combination is also known as "the claw.") Repeat command to toggle.

Right-clicking on a Track Insert button will bring up a menu listing various insert options, such as Bypass, Make Inactive, Automation Safe, and a sub-menu for Automation Dialog.

Insert Status Display

There are a number of display conditions indicating the current status of the insert:

- **Active, unmuted; plug-in window open.** The Insert button is white with black text.
- **Active, unmuted.** The Insert button is light gray with black text.
- **Active, muted; window open.** The Insert button is light blue with white text.
- **Active, muted.** The Insert button is blue with white text.
- **Clipped.** Regardless of mute state, text is red, plug-in meter shows red clip indicator.
- **Inactive.** The Insert button assumes track color, with black text in italics. When opened, the plug-in window will display the message "Plug-in Inactive."

Clear Clip Indicator

To clear the clip indicator, click on a red clip indicator, or press Option + C to clear all clips.

Insert Order

Inserts process in series, so think carefully about the order in which you add your plug-ins. Every plug-in you introduce will have an effect on every other plug-in downstream. While there is no *best* way, there is a *commonsense* way to order your plug-ins. Let's have a look at the order for vocal processing, for example:

- **Insert A:** EQ 3 1-Band
- **Insert B:** Compressor/Limiter Dyn 3
- **Insert C:** EQ 3 7-Band

    As always, your mileage may vary, but here's the reasoning behind this method:

- Filter unwanted frequency content *first*. That way your compressor doesn't have to respond to popped *p*'s or an overabundance of breath noise.
- Compress the vocal a moderate amount in order to control its place in the mix balance, dynamically speaking.
- Perform your EQ shaping after the dynamics have been tamed, and you will have a more consistent sound to work with. Plus, you won't accidentally be tripping the compressor with the +12 dB @ 16 kHz that you added to get the singer to sound breathy.

    You will notice that no delay or reverb plug-ins have been inserted directly into the vocal track. Using time-based effects directly on a track makes it much harder to control the level of the track in the mix and to control the balance of effect to dry vocal as well. It also increases latency dramatically for that track. Instead, take a moment to create an Aux bus in order to use delay and reverb as parallel-processed effects rather than series-processed. You will have more control over the effect, and your vocals will sound much more distinct using this technique.

An additional benefit of using Pro Tools Aux busses to administer effects is the obvious saving of CPU cycles. If you have 48 tracks of audio—each with its own reverb plug-in—you will be using much too much processing power to achieve your mixing goals. If one reverb isn't enough, create 2, or 4, or even 10 Aux busses to fulfill your reverb-drenched sonic fantasies. Better *10* than *48*. It's much easier to manage settings for a few reverbs than it is for a few *dozen*.

I hope this clarifies insert use and gives you solid techniques for maximizing your resources while striving for the best possible sound in your mixes.

Insert Output Format

Plug-ins can be configured in mono or stereo, but remember that because insert processing is done in series, inserting a stereo plug-in after a mono plug-in automatically makes all downstream inserts into stereo. You do not have the option of inserting a mono plug-in after a stereo plug-in.

There are three channel formats for plug-ins:
- mono-in/mono-out
- mono-in/stereo-out
- stereo-in/stereo-out

Note: some plug-ins come in multi-mono versions rather than stereo or multi-channel; they will behave as stereo devices in your insert chain.

Moving Inserts

Simply drag the plug-in from the Insert pane on one track to the Insert pane on another track to move the inserted plug-in. All plug-in parameters will move along with the insert.

Copying Inserts

Option + Drag the assigned insert to another Insert pane, whether on the same track or another. This is the fastest way to duplicate settings on an insert or plug-in.

Deleting Inserts

Click on the Insert pane you wish to delete or clear. The first choice in the drop-down menu will be "no insert." Click on this command to delete the insert and its settings from that Insert slot.

Note: You cannot undo this operation. Save your session before deleting anything you may wish to change your mind about.

Using Hardware Inserts

If you have favorite pieces of signal-processing equipment that you would like to use in the Pro Tools environment, you can use hardware inserts to connect your gear on individual tracks or sub-mixes. You must use corresponding inputs and outputs on your I/O to send and receive using the hardware inserts. For example, if you are sending signal out of the Pro Tools hardware inserts on output channels 3 and 4, you must return the processed signal to input channels 3 and 4.

Using Delay Compensation with Hardware Inserts

Delay Compensation can be applied to hardware inserts using the H/W Insert Delay page in I/O Setup. Here's how:
- Access the Setup menu and select I/O.
- Click on the H/W Insert Delay tab.
- Type the delay value (in milliseconds) into the input field where you have connected your hardware insert.

Calculating Delay When Using Hardware Inserts

Check the user's manual for the device you are about to connect; there may be a processing delay value listed in the specs. If that info is not available, you can use Pro Tools to determine your hardware delay. This is a bit of a process, but well worth the time invested. Follow these steps:

Step 1: Enable ADC.

Step 2: Set the Timeline Scale to measure minutes/seconds.

Step 3: Create two mono audio tracks.

Step 4: On the first track, create a short burst of tone using an oscillator plug-in. Alternately, use an audio file with an obvious visible beginning, such as a snare drum hit.

Step 5: Use a hardware insert on track 2.

Step 6: Bus the track 1 output to the input of track 2, and arm track 2 for recording.

Step 7: Record the test tone or other audio from track 1 onto track 2.

Step 8: Zoom in, and measure the distance between the beginning of the audio on track 1 and the beginning of the audio on track 2, using your Cursor tool to highlight the clip.

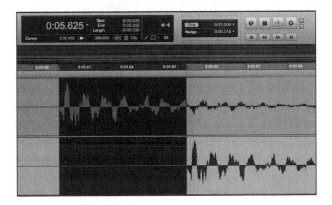

The resulting difference is the round-trip delay time of your external processor. This is also the value you will enter into the H/W Insert Delay page.

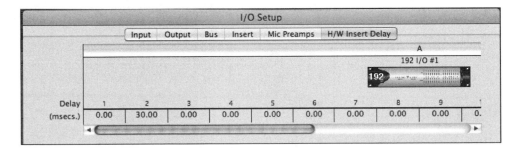

Remember, any added external processing will use additional voices and introduce latency.

Sends

- Pro Tools gives you ten sends per track in two banks of five each, A–E and F–J. These can be accessed from either the Edit or Mix windows, or from the send's own pop-up window.

- Sends are available in mono, stereo, or multi-channel on all audio tracks, Auxiliary Inputs, and instrument tracks.

- Pro Tools sends can be configured pre- or post-fader, much like an analog console.

- Sends are used for parallel processing; returns are audible in addition to the un-effected audio.

  Note: A send must return to the mixer via audio track, Auxiliary Input, or instrument track in order to be audible in Pro Tools.

  Send level, pan, and mute can be set to follow group assignments. In other words, if you change the send parameters for one member of a group, all members' sends will change in relation.

Common Uses for Sends Include:

- Send audio to a real-time effect plug-in or hardware insert for processing—reverb or delay, for example.
- Creating a separate mix or sub-mix. Drum or vocal sub-mixes would be examples of sub-mixes you would use regularly.
- Creating one or more headphone mixes that are separate from the main monitor mix.
- Sending audio to a plug-in key input.

Assigning a Send to a Track

- Enable Sends View in the Edit or Mix windows. For example, choose View > Edit Window Views > Inserts A–E.
- Click the Sends A–E pane of the track on which you would like to add the send. Select which output or bus destination you would like to send signal to. You may assign a send to a mono or stereo bus or output.
- Send level can be adjusted from the send level fader that pops up when you click on a send.

Send View Options

- The default view for sends is by bank (A–E and F–J). The number of sends displayed is related to the height of the track being viewed.
- You can set your send View options to display one send at a time (instead of five at a time) with send meter and all send controls visible all the time. To display Send A in the track send column, choose View > Sends A–E > Send A. From this pane, you can choose to view other sends from the drop-down menu.

- To return to all-sends view, simply choose View > Sends A–E > Assignments, or View > Sends F–J > Assignments as desired.

Send Status Display

There are a number of display conditions indicating the current status of the send:
- **Active, unmuted; window open.** The Send button is white with black text.
- **Active, unmuted.** The Send button is light gray with black text.
- **Active, muted; window open.** The Send button is light blue with white text.
- **Active, muted.** The Send button is dark blue with white text.
- **Inactive.** The Send button assumes track color, with black text in italics. When opened, all controls in the Send window will be grayed out.
- **Clipped.** Regardless of state, text is red; Send meter shows red clip indicator.

  To clear clip indicator, click on a red clip indicator, or press Option + C to clear all clips.

Opening Multiple Send Windows

Pro Tools normally allows you to have one Send window open at a time. It may be convenient for you to have more than one Send window open at once, in which case you can Shift + Click on the Send button to open a Send window and keep it open on the desktop. Use the same technique to open more Send windows. You can also click the red Target button on open Send windows to keep them open. To close these windows, click on the red Close button in the upper left corner of the Send window.

Create and Assign a New Track from a Send Pane

Using this feature, you can create and define a new send, create and define a new destination, and name the track, all in a single operation. Here's how to do it:
- From any active track, click on a send, and scroll down to the option named "new track…"
- The "new track…" dialog window will pop up, offering you the option to select send width (from mono and stereo through 7.1), the type of destination (Aux Input, Audio Track, or Instrument Track), choose samples/ticks, and name the destination track as well.

- If you click the button marked Create next to Current Track, then click Create, your new destination track will show up in the track list immediately below the track in which you selected the send.

  This is a big timesaver over the old multi-step process, but know that you can still assign sends and create destinations in separate steps if you prefer.

Master Faders

Whether or not you create a Master Fader on your virtual console, it *is* present, and the main output of your mix goes through it. Adding a Master Fader gives you a knob and the ability to make quick and easy adjustments to the final gain stage output.

Note: Adding a Master Fader does not change the resolution of your mix, even on fades—if it's a 24-bit session it will remain a 24-bit mix all the way down to <->infinity on the fader.

Master Faders Do Not Use Excessive DSP Resources

A Master Fader track gives you an opportunity to meter and control your mix *post-fader* so you know whether or not you're clipping the mixer output.

Creating a Master Fader for Stereo Master Volume Control:

- Using the Create New Track dialog (Shift + Command + N), create a new stereo Master Fader using the pull-down menus.

- Set the output for each track to the main audio output path, usually outputs 1 and 2 of your main hardware interface.
- Set the output of the Master Fader to the main output path.

Creating a Master Fader for Sub-Master Input Trim:

- Using the Create New Track dialog (Shift + Command + N), create a new stereo Auxiliary Input track.
- Bus the output of the desired tracks to the input of the Auxiliary Input track.
- Create a stereo Master Fader; assign the output to the same bus that feeds the Aux In track.

Inserting Plug-ins on the Master Fader

This is the same operation as inserting a send on a track. Click the Send window and select from the drop-down menu.

Uses for a Master Fader:

- Control and process output mixes.
- Monitor/meter outputs, busses, or hardware outputs.
- Control sub-mix levels.
- Control effects send levels.
- Control the level of bussed tracks (sub-masters).
- Apply dither and other effects to entire mixes.

Clearing Clipped Signal Indicators

- You can clear a signal clip indicator on a visible track meter by clicking the red clip indicator.
- Clear all clip indicators by pressing Option + C.

Organizing Your Tracks

Track layout in Pro Tools is mainly based on traditional music production techniques developed for use with analog multi-track tape on analog mixing consoles. A common method is to order your tracks in the Edit window from top to bottom beginning with the drums, then bass, followed by chordal instruments (keys, guitars, and so forth), vocals, and ending at the bottom with effects returns and finally the Master Fader. If you think ahead to the mix, you can begin to organize and structure the tracks in your session to make it easier for you to move into the mixing process once all of the tracks have been recorded and edited. In the Mix window, the tracks will appear from left to right, beginning with drums, bass, chord instruments, vocals, and effects return tracks. This emulates an analog console layout and places the vocal tracks closest to the Master section of the console. The theory is that you'll be spending more time mixing the vocal tracks, and keeping them in the center of the console also puts you consistently in the parallax of the speakers.

You will develop your own scheme for laying out virtual console tracks based on your work flow, the type of project, and your experience with template layouts.

Edit Window Layout

Info Display

You can customize the information displayed in the Edit window by selecting from the drop-down menu at the top of the screen (View > Edit Window Views). From here you can choose which of the following to display:

- Comments
- Mic Preamps
- Instruments
- Inserts A–E
- Inserts F–J
- Sends A–E
- Sends F–J
- I/O
- Real-Time Properties
- Track Color

Note: These selections are also available from a drop-down menu located on the top left of the Edit window just below the Rulers display.

Displaying Rulers

Depending on the time-base and editing style of choice, you can select the rulers best suited for your editing operation. You can also display Markers, Tempo, Meter, and other song-specific parameters in the Ruler display. To access these options, select the drop-down menu: View > Rulers.

Group Assignments

At the lower-left corner of the Mix window, you will find an area titled Groups. The default setting includes just one group—All—which, when highlighted, ties all tracks together for editing commands. Cut, Paste, Copy, Move—whatever commands you assign to the global group will affect all tracks. You can add up to 104 groups of tracks of your choosing by selecting the Name field for each track and typing Command + G, then naming the group. It will then be added to the list of groups and can be turned on or off by toggling the state within the Groups window.

You should create a new group for every instrument that occupies more than one track. In a typical rock band recording, you might have a group for each instrument, which will make mixing an easier task. For example:

- Drums
- Bass
- Guitars (GTR)
- Keyboards
- Background Vocals (BGV)
- Main Vocal (VOX)

Having a group assignment for each species of tracks will make it much easier to balance levels between instruments, perform edits, and engage automation functions. All members of the group will respond to a parameter change on one member track.

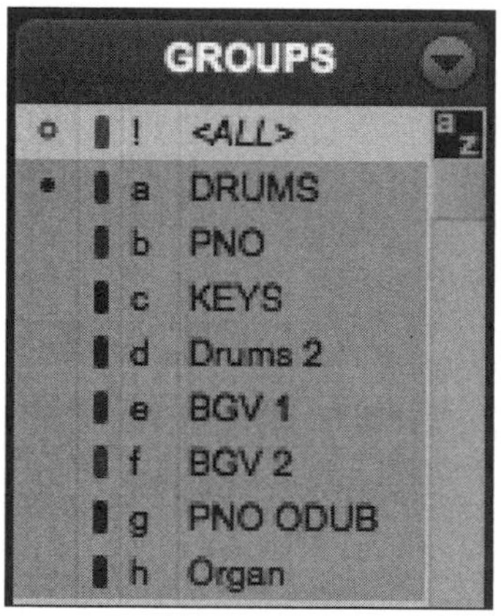

Note: the Group function can be temporarily suspended for an individual track simply by pressing the Control key and adjusting the parameter you wish to change. Releasing the Control key returns parameter adjustments to their group state.

View Tracks

The Tracks View pane lives on the left-hand side of the Edit window and shows/hides tracks in the Edit and Mix windows based on selection or type. There is a drop-down menu in the Tracks pane to allow access to these selections, as well as sorting options.

The Tracks pane can be shown or hidden by accessing the drop-down menu View > Other Displays > Track List.

You can number the tracks in the Tracks pane as well, which is really handy for finding your way among a mix containing 96 tracks. Select from the drop-down menu View > Track Number.

Hiding Tracks

If you have chosen to view the Tracks window on the left-hand side of the Edit window page, you now have the option to modify the number of tracks viewed in the Edit window at any time. Simply click the dot icon next to a track name to alternately hide or make it visible.

This is a handy function if you have a number of input tracks you are not currently using. Or if you have recorded alternate takes or solos and don't need the info in your Edit or Mix windows, you may remove them from view. Keep in mind, hidden tracks will still play and utilize output voices. If you truly want a track to be silent, you should mute all clips within the track, make the track inactive, or delete the track from the sequence. If you choose the latter method, be sure to make a copy of your session and rename it so you don't lose any track info permanently.

Note: Group commands still apply to hidden tracks, whether or not you can see them. Don't be surprised when that muted scratch vocal track makes a mysterious and unwanted reappearance after you unmute a visible track in the group. When in doubt, make a track inactive first, then hide it. For hiding multiple tracks, there is a Hide Inactive Tracks command within the Tracks column drop-down menu.

Grid Settings

If the song you are recording lends itself to a consistent tempo, try recording to a click track. Pro Tools will generate a click track simply by selecting the "Create click track" command from the Track window. Then select a tempo in the Transport window, or tap the tempo using the "T" key. It's super easy to have all of your editing commands conform to precise bar and beat lines in Grid mode. Find the Grid pane at the top of the Edit Window, and click the arrow. This allows you to access and modify grid settings. Typically, you will resolve the grid to quarter notes when in Bar/Beat mode, though this will depend on the tempo of the song and complexity of the edit you are performing. Set your Edit mode to Grid or Relative Grid so that everything you edit or move will snap to the beat.

If your song was not recorded with a click track, you can still use Grid mode, but it will not relate to the tempo of your song. In which case, I would suggest setting the grid resolution to minutes/seconds and using it for elapsed time reference only. Use SLIP mode for editing, in this case.

Suggestion: You can guesstimate tempo using the Tap Tempo mode in the Metronome pane of your Transport window by turning the Conductor track off, highlighting the BPM rate, then tapping the "T" key in time with the music.

Nudge Settings

As in the description of Grid settings above, go to the Nudge Settings pane in the Edit window and click the arrow. This gives you access to the nudge resolution. Again, if you have recorded your song to a click, then using Bar/Beat mode in the Nudge Settings window will allow you to move clips or notes in beats or fractions of a beat. This can be really handy for editing MIDI performances.

Whether recorded to a click track or not, I leave my Nudge mode set on minutes/seconds and use 10 ms as the base nudge resolution. I have found that adjusting timing on performance recorded as audio tracks requires much finer resolution, and may only need to be moved 10 or 20 ms in order to rectify a late hit or a missed downbeat. The following keys access nudge commands:

- The comma key (,) moves the selected clip or note 1 increment earlier.
- The period key (.) moves the selected clip or note 1 increment later.
- The "M" key (m) moves the selected clip or note 10 increments earlier.
- The forward slash key (/) moves the selected clip or note 10 increments later.
- If your nudge resolution is set to 10 ms, then the comma and period keys move in 10 ms increments, and the "M" and forward slash keys move in 100 ms increments.

Color Palette

Changing the color assignments on elements of your screen layout will help you quickly locate and identify tracks, clips, markers, or groups of tracks. Sometimes the drums just look cooler in green. Either way, the Color Palette gives you the option to organize by color.

- Double-click in the color bar area left of the track name in the Edit window, also at the very top of the channel strip in the Mix window. (Or select Window > Color Palette). This will bring up the Color Palette window, which allows you to choose colors for tracks, clips, groups, and markers.
- Note: If the Marker option is grayed out, you will need to go to the Preferences window, click on the Display tab, then click the Always Display Marker Colors button.
- Select the track(s), clips, group, or marker you'd like to modify. The currently selected color will be indicated by a highlighted swatch in the Color Palette window. You can select a new color by clicking the desired color swatch.
- The Undo command (Command + Z) gets you back to the previously selected color. You can also click the Default button in the Color Palette window to return to the factory setting for the selected item.

Memory Locations/Markers

Memory Location Markers are a great way to identify and navigate quickly to positions within your session. This will be a huge timesaver when working on specific sections of a song during overdubs. Use markers to identify the beginning of a take, a section of a song, or an event within a song that you'll need to locate again easily. Markers are numbered sequentially as you add them. To display the Markers ruler, select from the View menu: View > Rulers > Markers.

There are four ways to bring up the New Memory Location dialog. First, locate to the desired point in the timeline, or highlight a clip. Then do one of the following:

- Press the Enter key on the numeric keypad.
- Control + Click in the Markers ruler near the top of the Edit window.

- In the Memory Locations window, Command + Click.
- Click on the "+" sign in the Markers ruler.

As you create a new marker, the New Memory Location window will reveal a number of options, including typing a marker name, changing the marker number, selecting Time Properties, and setting General Properties.

Marker Memory Location relates to a particular point in the timeline.

Selection Memory Location relates to a user-designated edit selection in the timeline.

- Select or highlight a clip in the timeline.
- Create a Memory Location, then hit Enter to add marker.
- Click the Selection button, then click OK.
- The clip selection is stored along with the other Memory Location parameters.

General Properties Memory Location relates to a set of session settings that can be stored and recalled.

- Storing or recalling General Properties data can include screen views, zoom settings, pre- and post-roll times, track show/hide status, track height, and enabled Edit/Mix groups. This does not necessarily require location information.
- This can be handy when viewing the drum kit or vocals during editing, or for recalling your Master Fader metering layout during the mixdown process.
- To store these details, set up the screen view to your satisfaction, then check the boxes corresponding to the information you wish to save.
- See the section below on Window Configurations to set up specific window layouts and views, which can then be recalled in the General Properties pane.

Each session can store up to 999 Memory Locations.

- These are stored and displayed in the Memory Locations window accessed by typing Command + 5 on the main keyboard, or by accessing the Window > Memory Locations window.
- Memory Locations can be recalled, modified, created, and deleted from this window as well.
- Command + Click to add a new marker.
- Option + Click to delete a marker.
- You can sort, edit, and renumber markers in this window as well.

To locate a specific marker, type its number on the numeric keypad in this sequence: decimal point, (number), decimal point.

Locating to Marker 2 looks like this: .2.

You can also click on the Marker icon in the Marker ruler of the Edit window or in the Memory Locations window. You will find a list of your markers in the Memory Location window. Markers can be moved by grabbing the Marker icon in the Marker ruler and dragging it to the desired location.

Note: Markers will snap to Grid settings if moved while Grid mode is selected.
Common section marker names include:
- Intro
- Verse (or verse 1, verse 2, and so forth)
- Chorus (or chorus 1, chorus 2, and so forth)
- Solo
- Bridge
- Breakdown
- Modulation
- Outchorus
- Coda
- And any other section names that might apply to the piece you are working on.

Note: Use the Enter key on the numeric keypad to drop markers at the beginning of every new section while recording. You can go back and name the markers/sections later, as well as adjusting their precise location. Having these rough markers placed will be a tremendous timesaver when trying to locate sections within a song.

Another note: It's efficient (not to mention impressive) when a client asks to hear the bass line in the second chorus, and you can locate that section immediately because you had the forethought to drop a marker there during the recording of basic tracks.

Yet another note: I like to add a marker at the very beginning and the very end of the song as well; this helps to easily identify the length of the entire song when it comes time to bounce the mix to disk.

To Delete a Marker:
- In the Marker ruler, drag the Marker icon down until it turns into a Trash Can icon. When you release the Mouse button, the Marker will be deleted.
- In the Memory Locations window, Option + Click on a marker to delete it from the list.
- These operations can be undone (Command + Z).

Window Configurations

This tool allows you to set up a screen view for each selected operation you wish to use, save it as a Window Configuration, and instantly recall the screen view.

Note: This is really handy for getting a focused view of just the tracks that need editing, such as drums or vocals, without having to reconfigure your screen manually for each operation.

How to Create a Window Configuration

Open the Window Configuration window by locating the drop-down menu Windows > Configurations > Window Configurations List, or pressing Command + Option + J.

Start by making a new Window Configuration setting named "Default" with your basic window layout of choice. You can add comments for your reference in the field provided. When you click OK, it will be saved to position 1 in your Window Configurations list. Use this as the main layout for editing or mixing.

Now let's make a new window layout featuring just the drum tracks:
- Open the Clips and open the Strip Silence window (Command + U).

will naturally choose the method that is fastest or most efficient. With some practice, you will find that a lot of these operations become muscle memory as a result of having used them so often. Saving, for instance. You should save your work often, and the fastest way to do this by far is to use the keyboard to type Command + S. Most DAW users can find that command in the dark, and you should too. As I tell my students, only save if you like what you've done and want to keep it. (In other words: save everything all the time.)

Playlists

If you have recorded tracks with alternate playlists, you should review them to be sure you're using the master take. View alternate playlists by clicking the Track View Selector button in the Edit window, then selecting playlists. This will open a playlist lane beneath each track showing you all takes for each track.

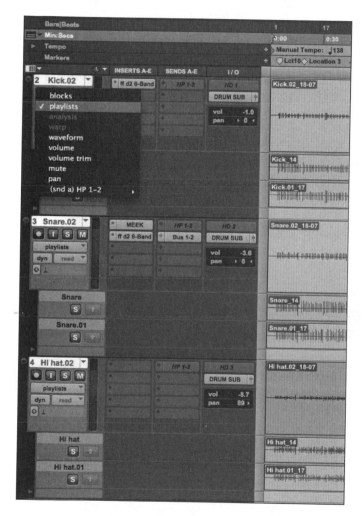

You can also view a playlist by clicking the Track Name button and selecting the number of the playlist you wish to view.

- Open the New Configuration menu from the main Windows menu (Windows > Configurations > New Configuration…) or from the drop-down menu in the Window Configurations window.

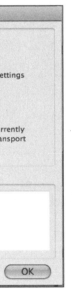

- Select Window Layout and type the name "Drum Kit View" into the Name field. Press OK, and this will be saved to Window Configuration 2.

Now we'll test the system; recall your Default Window Configuration by typing Period (.), one (1), Asterisk (*):

.1*

This should recall your original default window layout. Next, type:

.2*

This should restore your "Drum Kit View" layout.

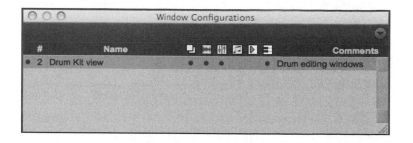

Note: If you have selected Auto-Update Active Configuration from either drop-down menu, changes to the active view will be saved with the Window Configuration. The number of the currently selected Window Configuration will be displayed in parentheses next to the Window menu at the top of the screen.

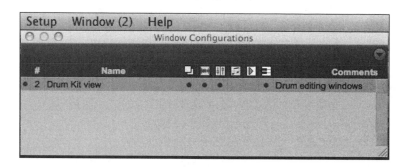

I suggest leaving this item unchecked unless you need to modify your view, or you may accidentally overwrite your configurations. There is no Undo function for this operation.

To delete a Window Configuration, select the subject configuration from the Window Configuration page and choose "Delete (name of configuration)" from the drop-down menu. Another way to delete the setting is to Option + Click on the subject configuration in the Window Configuration menu. It will then be permanently deleted.

Your Window Configuration settings will be saved with your session. Window Configuration settings can be imported from other sessions using the Import Window Configurations command in the Import Session Data > Import Options dialog.

Mix Window Layout

Many of the functions and views in the Mix window are also available in the Edit window, and are accessible from the same menus.

Memory Locations

The Memory Locations window allows you to see all of the markers you've added to the session, to edit the data stored in each, and to view them in order of creation or numerical sequence.

Window Configurations

This window allows you to create and store custom window views for instant recall. This can be superhandy when editing and mixing, because you can instantly focus your attention (and screen real estate) on just the tracks you are editing and hide the remainder until you need them again. These configurations can be stored as memory locations too, giving you nearly instant access to single or multiple track views.

Transport Window

The Transport Window shows basic transport controls (Return to zero [RTZ], Rewind, Fast Forward, Go to End [GTE], Stop, Play, and Record buttons), counters, and some MIDI controls. It can also be configured to show Pre/Post Roll, Count-off, Tempo, and Metronome settings, as well as enabling the Tempo Ruler (or Conductor track).

While these commands can always be accessed at the top of the Edit and Mix windows, the Transport window can be a floating window as well. This allows you to position it on your monitor screen wherever you may need it. The quick access key command is Command + 1 on the numeric keypad. See more info on the Transport window in a separate chapter of this book.

Editing Operations

Okay, now that we have some of the mechanics squared away, let's get down to editing the tracks. As we get into practical application of the tools and techniques presented here, you will quickly see that there are at least five different ways to do everything in Pro Tools. Or so it would seem. This is not designed to make you crazy but rather to give you options at every turn. If you know at least three ways to solve a problem, you

Note: Playlist views subscribe to group assignments, so if you switch playlists on a drums group, for example, the view of all member tracks will switch as well. By activating All in the Groups pane, all tracks will switch their playlist views when one is changed.

Duplicating Tracks

You can duplicate tracks by selecting Track > Duplicate…(or Shift + Option + D), then completing the instructions and clicking OK.

Note: You cannot undo this operation. You will have to delete the track manually if you want it gone.

To delete a track: Highlight the track name to be deleted, select Track > Delete…; a pop-up window will then ask you if you're sure, because there are active clips within the track. Click OK to delete. You cannot undo this operation either.

Cleaning Tracks

Whether you recorded every instrument yourself or inherited tracks from other engineers, you will find it necessary to edit portions of the tracks if you find them to be noisy or otherwise unusable. Pro Tools gives you a number of ways to deal with the job of cleanup.

Strip Silence

Pro Tools has a handy function called Strip Silence that eliminates sections of a clip falling below a user-defined threshold level. If you select a clip and open Strip Silence (Command + U), you will see a dialog box giving you access to four adjustable parameters allowing you to define "silence." As you adjust the Strip Threshold, you will see the clip view divided up into smaller and more numerous sub-clips. Use this to determine the minimum amplitude at which a new clip will be created. The other parameters—Minimum Strip Duration, Clip Start Pad, and Clip End Pad—allow you to force durations onto the new clips to be created. In other words, you can set a minimum duration, or extend each clip end by "adding" a few milliseconds of silence before the clip start time. This is a great way to remove noise between tom hits, headphone leakage between vocal lines, or amp hum between guitar lines.

Click the Strip command button to complete the operation once your selections have been fine-tuned.

Note: You can always undo this operation later in the process by selecting all the stripped clips and pressing Command + H to heal the track, thereby restoring it to its original state before the Strip Silence operation was performed (as you long as you didn't move the sub-clips or change the timing).

Noise Gates

Another way to mute noisy tracks is to use a Noise Gate plug-in on the offending track. Noise gates can be set to reduce track volume (or even be completely silenced) when signal falls below the gate threshold. Gate attack, release, and duration can be set to your specification in real-time, tailoring the ADSR of the gating function.

Frequency-dependent gates allow you to focus in on the part of the spectrum where, say, a snare drum lives, and use that specific part of the frequency spectrum to open the snare gate. Regardless of how hard the drummer is whacking the floor tom. This is also superhandy for drums, horns, noisy amplifiers, audience mics, and so forth.

Gates can be "keyed" or triggered by audio from another track, giving you the option to have the kick drum control the opening of the gate on a bass guitar, for example.

Gates can also be used to trigger a reverb send or return for heightened dramatic effect, opening when the vocalist sings above a particular volume level.

The more you mess with gates, the more practical uses you will discover.

Manual Editing

There will be times when using Strip Silence or a noise gate just doesn't give you the control you need to clean up your tracks. An example would be cleaning tom tom tracks on the recording of a drum kit. There's usually too much going on in a drum kit to use Strip Silence, since the background noise on tom tracks typically doesn't drop low enough to consistently differentiate a tom hit from a snare hit. A noise gate would suffer from the same false triggering issues and is not smart enough to respond to an overlapping cymbal crash with a natural-sounding decay time. The solution is to clean your tracks manually using Pro Tools editing functions to separate and mute unwanted clips.

Once you have isolated a tom hit, separate the clip (B). Next, highlight the clip before the tom hit, and cut (X), delete (Delete), or mute it (Command + M). Do this operation for every tom hit on the track(s).

Now you can fine-tune the duration of each tom hit clip and fade in or out as the context of the performance dictates—i.e., if tom hit one occurs without any cymbal bleed, you can draw a 500 ms fade after the waveform dissipates and it'll sound pretty natural in the mix. If there is a cymbal crash concurrently with a tom hit, you may need to extend the end of the tom hit clip by two seconds, then draw a one-second fade-out. Do this with every tom hit on all tom tracks, and you should have a cleaner sounding drum kit overall, as the toms usually contribute noise and tonal coloration that takes away from the sonic quality of the drum kit.

Mute Clip vs. Delete Clip

Let's say you've decided to invest the time in editing your tracks manually. Do you delete the unwanted clips, or do you simply mute them? I do either or both, depending on the situation. If there is nothing but noise, hiss, or hum in the space between actual playing or singing, I will delete the unwanted bits. Likewise, if the track is silent for most of a take, I will truncate the clip(s) to include audible parts only.

If a performance is to be edited out—for content or for mistakes—I like to mute the clip. This grays out the clip but allows me to see if there are still waveforms present, and gives me the option to easily bring those clips back into the mix if I want them. Especially useful if I've edited a tom track and temporarily lost a subtle fill.

- Open the New Configuration menu from the main Windows menu (Windows > Configurations > New Configuration…) or from the drop-down menu in the Window Configurations window.

- Select Window Layout and type the name "Drum Kit View" into the Name field. Press OK, and this will be saved to Window Configuration 2.

  Now we'll test the system; recall your Default Window Configuration by typing Period (.), one (1), Asterisk (*):

  .1*

  This should recall your original default window layout. Next, type:

  .2*

This should restore your "Drum Kit View" layout.

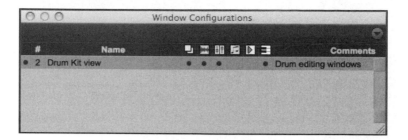

Note: If you have selected Auto-Update Active Configuration from either drop-down menu, changes to the active view will be saved with the Window Configuration. The number of the currently selected Window Configuration will be displayed in parentheses next to the Window menu at the top of the screen.

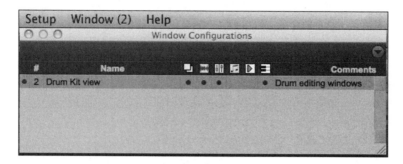

I suggest leaving this item unchecked unless you need to modify your view, or you may accidentally overwrite your configurations. There is no Undo function for this operation.

To delete a Window Configuration, select the subject configuration from the Window Configuration page and choose "Delete (name of configuration)" from the drop-down menu. Another way to delete the setting is to Option + Click on the subject configuration in the Window Configuration menu. It will then be permanently deleted.

Your Window Configuration settings will be saved with your session. Window Configuration settings can be imported from other sessions using the Import Window Configurations command in the Import Session Data > Import Options dialog.

Mix Window Layout

Many of the functions and views in the Mix window are also available in the Edit window, and are accessible from the same menus.

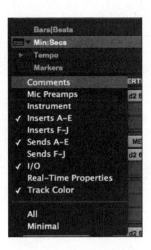

Memory Locations

The Memory Locations window allows you to see all of the markers you've added to the session, to edit the data stored in each, and to view them in order of creation or numerical sequence.

Window Configurations

This window allows you to create and store custom window views for instant recall. This can be superhandy when editing and mixing, because you can instantly focus your attention (and screen real estate) on just the tracks you are editing and hide the remainder until you need them again. These configurations can be stored as memory locations too, giving you nearly instant access to single or multiple track views.

Transport Window

The Transport Window shows basic transport controls (Return to zero [RTZ], Rewind, Fast Forward, Go to End [GTE], Stop, Play, and Record buttons), counters, and some MIDI controls. It can also be configured to show Pre/Post Roll, Count-off, Tempo, and Metronome settings, as well as enabling the Tempo Ruler (or Conductor track).

While these commands can always be accessed at the top of the Edit and Mix windows, the Transport window can be a floating window as well. This allows you to position it on your monitor screen wherever you may need it. The quick access key command is Command + 1 on the numeric keypad. See more info on the Transport window in a separate chapter of this book.

Editing Operations

Okay, now that we have some of the mechanics squared away, let's get down to editing the tracks. As we get into practical application of the tools and techniques presented here, you will quickly see that there are at least five different ways to do everything in Pro Tools. Or so it would seem. This is not designed to make you crazy but rather to give you options at every turn. If you know at least three ways to solve a problem, you will naturally choose the method that is fastest or most efficient. With some practice, you will find that a lot of these operations become muscle memory as a result of having used them so often. Saving, for instance. You should save your work often, and the fastest way to do this by far is to use the keyboard to type Command + S. Most DAW users can find that command in the dark, and you should too. As I tell my students, only save if you like what you've done and want to keep it. (In other words: save everything all the time.)

Playlists

If you have recorded tracks with alternate playlists, you should review them to be sure you're using the master take. View alternate playlists by clicking the Track View Selector button in the Edit window, then selecting playlists. This will open a playlist lane beneath each track showing you all takes for each track.

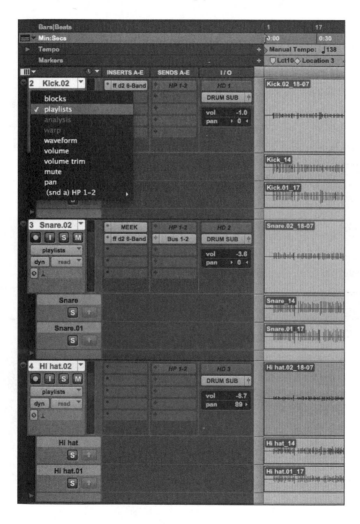

You can also view a playlist by clicking the Track Name button and selecting the number of the playlist you wish to view.

Note: Playlist views subscribe to group assignments, so if you switch playlists on a drums group, for example, the view of all member tracks will switch as well. By activating All in the Groups pane, all tracks will switch their playlist views when one is changed.

Duplicating Tracks

You can duplicate tracks by selecting Track > Duplicate…(or Shift + Option + D), then completing the instructions and clicking OK.

Note: You cannot undo this operation. You will have to delete the track manually if you want it gone.

To delete a track: Highlight the track name to be deleted, select Track > Delete…; a pop-up window will then ask you if you're sure, because there are active clips within the track. Click OK to delete. You cannot undo this operation either.

Cleaning Tracks

Whether you recorded every instrument yourself or inherited tracks from other engineers, you will find it necessary to edit portions of the tracks if you find them to be noisy or otherwise unusable. Pro Tools gives you a number of ways to deal with the job of cleanup.

Strip Silence

Pro Tools has a handy function called Strip Silence that eliminates sections of a clip falling below a user-defined threshold level. If you select a clip and open Strip Silence (Command + U), you will see a dialog box giving you access to four adjustable parameters allowing you to define "silence." As you adjust the Strip Threshold, you will see the clip view divided up into smaller and more numerous sub-clips. Use this to determine the minimum amplitude at which a new clip will be created. The other parameters—Minimum Strip Duration, Clip Start Pad, and Clip End Pad—allow you to force durations onto the new clips to be created. In other words, you can set a minimum duration, or extend each clip end by "adding" a few milliseconds of silence before the clip start time. This is a great way to remove noise between tom hits, headphone leakage between vocal lines, or amp hum between guitar lines.

Click the Strip command button to complete the operation once your selections have been fine-tuned.

Note: You can always undo this operation later in the process by selecting all the stripped clips and pressing Command + H to heal the track, thereby restoring it to its original state before the Strip Silence operation was performed (as you long as you didn't move the sub-clips or change the timing).

Noise Gates

Another way to mute noisy tracks is to use a Noise Gate plug-in on the offending track. Noise gates can be set to reduce track volume (or even be completely silenced) when signal falls below the gate threshold. Gate attack, release, and duration can be set to your specification in real-time, tailoring the ADSR of the gating function.

Frequency-dependent gates allow you to focus in on the part of the spectrum where, say, a snare drum lives, and use that specific part of the frequency spectrum to open the snare gate. Regardless of how hard the drummer is whacking the floor tom. This is also superhandy for drums, horns, noisy amplifiers, audience mics, and so forth.

Gates can be "keyed" or triggered by audio from another track, giving you the option to have the kick drum control the opening of the gate on a bass guitar, for example.

Gates can also be used to trigger a reverb send or return for heightened dramatic effect, opening when the vocalist sings above a particular volume level.

The more you mess with gates, the more practical uses you will discover.

Manual Editing

There will be times when using Strip Silence or a noise gate just doesn't give you the control you need to clean up your tracks. An example would be cleaning tom tom tracks on the recording of a drum kit. There's usually too much going on in a drum kit to use Strip Silence, since the background noise on tom tracks typically doesn't drop low enough to consistently differentiate a tom hit from a snare hit. A noise gate would suffer from the same false triggering issues and is not smart enough to respond to an overlapping cymbal crash with a natural-sounding decay time. The solution is to clean your tracks manually using Pro Tools editing functions to separate and mute unwanted clips.

Once you have isolated a tom hit, separate the clip (B). Next, highlight the clip before the tom hit, and cut (X), delete (Delete), or mute it (Command + M). Do this operation for every tom hit on the track(s).

Now you can fine-tune the duration of each tom hit clip and fade in or out as the context of the performance dictates—i.e., if tom hit one occurs without any cymbal bleed, you can draw a 500 ms fade after the waveform dissipates and it'll sound pretty natural in the mix. If there is a cymbal crash concurrently with a tom hit, you may need to extend the end of the tom hit clip by two seconds, then draw a one-second fade-out. Do this with every tom hit on all tom tracks, and you should have a cleaner sounding drum kit overall, as the toms usually contribute noise and tonal coloration that takes away from the sonic quality of the drum kit.

Mute Clip vs. Delete Clip

Let's say you've decided to invest the time in editing your tracks manually. Do you delete the unwanted clips, or do you simply mute them? I do either or both, depending on the situation. If there is nothing but noise, hiss, or hum in the space between actual playing or singing, I will delete the unwanted bits. Likewise, if the track is silent for most of a take, I will truncate the clip(s) to include audible parts only.

If a performance is to be edited out—for content or for mistakes—I like to mute the clip. This grays out the clip but allows me to see if there are still waveforms present, and gives me the option to easily bring those clips back into the mix if I want them. Especially useful if I've edited a tom track and temporarily lost a subtle fill.

Consolidating Clips

Once you have cleaned your tracks and made your final edits, you should consolidate a heavily edited track into a new contiguous clip by using the Consolidate command from the Edit menu at the top of the page. This serves to make a single file out of many edited clips, thereby conserving CPU and disk load. It also makes it much easier to keep track of files when it comes time to back up your session.

Note: While consolidating a clip does write a new file to disk, that file does not contain any of the underlying automation information or any of the plug-in or insert processing.

Summary of Key Commands

Operation	Key Command
Session Setup Menu	Command + 2 (numeric keypad)
Bypass Insert	Command + Click Insert button
Bypass All "A" Inserts	Option + Click "A" Insert button (or B, C, etc.)
Make Insert Inactive	Control + Command + Click Insert button
Make All "A" Inserts Inactive	Control + Option + Command + Click "A" Insert button
Clear Clip Indicator	Option + C
Copy Insert	Option + Drag to new Insert slot
Keep Send Window Open	Shift + Click Send button
Create New Track	Shift + Command + N
Import Session Data	Shift + Option + I
Import Audio	Shift + Command + I
Add Group	Select Tracks, then Command + G
Undo	Command + Z
New Memory Location	Enter (numeric keypad), Control + Click Marker ruler, Command + Click Memory Locations window
Memory Location Window	Command + 5 (main keyboard)
Delete Memory Location	Option + Click Marker
Go To Memory Location	.number. (e.g., .2. for marker 2) on the numeric keypad
Window Configurations	Command + Option + J
Strip Silence	Command + U
Transport	Command + 1 (numeric keypad)
Save	Command + S
Duplicate Track	Shift + Option + D
Heal Separation	Command + H
Separate Clip	B, or Command + E
Cut	X, or Command + X
Copy	C, or Command + C
Paste	V, or Command + V
Mute Clip	Command + M
Nudge Left	, (comma)
Nudge Right	. (period)
Nudge Left x10	M
Nudge Right x10	/ (forward slash)

Chapter 2 Review

1. Pro Tools now offers four levels of pan depth for varying degrees of stereo image accuracy when panning across the center position. These are ___ dB, ___dB, ___ dB, and ___ dB.

2. An Aux send is used to send a parallel _____ from a track to a bus for _____ to effects or outputs.

3. _____ -fader sends are used for headphone mixes, while _____ sends are used for effects sends.

4. Pro Tools allows you to use either software _____ or hardware inserts on each track. A hardware insert requires physical inputs and outputs on your audio _____ in order to connect _____ hardware.

5. Hardware inserts use additional _____ allocation and introduce _____.

6. _____ plug-ins are usually added to Aux Inputs, and _____ are routed from the tracks to the reverb plug-in. This saves processing horsepower.

7. Copying an insert or a send from one track to another is easily accomplished by using the _____ + _____ command to copy the insert or send with all settings intact.

8. Calculating hardware _____ in Pro Tools involves recording a small piece of audio through a _____ send/return path and comparing it with an undelayed sample.

9. Pro Tools gives you _____ sends and _____ inserts per track.

10. Creating a _____ gives you a control with which to vary the output level of your mix.

11. You can clear clip indicators by pressing the _____ + _____ key command.

12. To manipulate more than one track at once, create a _____ by selecting the desired members, then pressing the _____ + G keys.

13. Tap in a desired _____ using the "T" key.

14. You can access all of the basic session navigation controls, including Record and Play, using the _____ window.

15. Hiding tracks from within the Tracks window will remove them from the _____ and _____ Window views, but they will still be audible as long as they are active.

16. You can create very accurate edits using the Grid and Nudge settings. The Nudge key commands are the ___, ___, ___, and ___ keys, and they usually correspond to -10 x, -1 x, +1 x, and +10 x the nudge settings.

17. Use the _____ key on the numeric keypad to create a new marker. Each session can store up to _____ memory markers.

18. You can save your session by typing the key command _____ + ___.

19. The Pro Tools function used to remove sections of low-amplitude signal from within a clip is called _____.

20. Heavily edited clips can be combined to create a new file on disk using the _____ command from the File menu.

Chapter 3
PREPARING THE SESSION

Pre-Production

I firmly believe that an hour of pre-pro can save you 10 hours in editing/mixing, potentially even more than that. In the earlier discussion about what makes a recording sound good or bad, we covered the idea of using a pre-session technical checklist to be sure your equipment is in proper working order. Since every session is different, you should develop a detailed pre-production checklist to help you avoid potential pitfalls when the time comes to hit the red button and start recording. The list will be longer and more detailed when recording a group of musicians as opposed to a single performer, but a checklist is valuable all the same. Some of the questions may seem obvious, but if following a pre-op checklist helps surgeons to be more efficient and make fewer mistakes, then we engineers can do it too.

Recording a Band—Pre-Session Checklist

- What is the style of music?
- How many members are in the band?
- What is the instrumentation?
- What is the budget?
- Does the budget include expenses such as hiring additional musicians, mastering, duplication, or anything else?
- When does the project need to be finished?
- Is the same engineer recording/editing/mixing/mastering?
- Will the musicians all be playing at once or individually?
- Does the artist have demos of the songs you can listen to?
- What is the desired sonic outcome, for the band and for individual instruments? Is there a musical reference?
- What bit/sample rate will you be using?
- Who is providing the hard drives for this project, and who will ultimately be responsible for the data?
- What data settings will you be using?

We could do a chapter on each of these questions, but for now, answering the questions on this list will help shape the session and inform you about possible red flags before the band enters the studio.

Recording an Individual Performer

- What is the style of music?
- What is the instrumentation?
- What is the budget?
- Does the budget include expenses such as hiring additional musicians, mastering, duplication, or anything else?
- When does the project need to be finished?
- Is the same engineer recording/editing/mixing/mastering?
- Will the performer be working with loops, beats, or pre-recorded tracks?
- Does the artist have demos of the songs you can listen to?
- What is the desired sonic outcome; is there a musical reference?
- Who is providing the hard drives for this project, and who will ultimately be responsible for the data?
- What data settings will you be using?

The answers to these questions will shape the session and dictate the work flow. The more info you can get in advance of the session, the more efficiently you'll be able to work, and the smoother your session will proceed.

Session Basics

You will need to determine some important session settings before you can start recording. You can start a new Pro Tools session by choosing New Session from the File menu or by typing Command + N. You will then see a dialog box asking for you to select a series of settings for the session.

Let's walk through the options for building your Pro Tools session:

- Sample rate: 44.1 kHz, 48 kHz, 88.2 kHz, 96 kHz, 176.4 kHz, or 192 kHz.
- Bit depth: 16-bits or 24-bits.
- File format: AIFF or BWF (.WAV).

While you should always try to work at the highest quality settings, it's not always appropriate to work at 24-bit/192 kHz sample rate. For example, if you're working on audio for a game or a TV program, your ultimate delivery format may be 16-bit/44.1 kHz .WAV or 16-bit/48 kHz AIFF, respectively. While you can always convert your mix to a different standard while bouncing, you may find it more efficient from a work flow standpoint to build your session in the final delivery format. Also, working at higher bit/sample rates will increase the amount of hard drive space required to store the session data, will limit track counts within Pro Tools, and may affect system performance, depending on the capability of your machine. Here are some common delivery formats:

- Audio CD: 16-bit/44.1 kHz AIFF
- Audio DVD (DVD-A): 24-bit/96 kHz AIFF
- Video DVD (DVD): 16-bit/48 kHz AIFF
- TV: 16-bit/48 kHz AIFF
- Game authoring: 16-bit/44.1 kHz .WAV
- Online music distribution: 16-bit/44.1 kHz 128 kbps MP3 or AAC

Note: Pro Tools 11 now gives you the option to record/edit/mix in the MP3 file format, although this is not recommended. Pro Tools now allows you to use audio with different bit, sample, and/or format settings within the same session. You may need to convert your files before playing back or editing to ensure that all files match the selected bit, sample rate, and format of your session settings.

Working with Session Templates

When you build a new session in Pro Tools, you can choose from a number of pre-built session templates, which can save a lot of time in building a session from scratch, particularly if you are tracking a band with many inputs. You can also build your own templates based on previous sessions or your own particular work flow. To explore the session templates when starting a new session, choose New Session from the File menu, or type Command + N to bring up the New Session dialog. From here, you will be offered the option to choose templates from a drop-down menu to aid in building your new session. When recording live musicians, select a template from the Record + Mix category, based on the number of tracks you'll need. For example, the 24+FX Returns template features a pre-built session with 24 mono audio tracks with pre-assigned headphone, reverb, delay, and chorus Auxiliary sends, as well as Aux returns for the above. It also includes a Master Fader and a click track to complete the picture. If the session is MIDI-based, choose from the Music or Songwriter categories for an array of pre-built options.

The Template Selection window gives you the ability to select audio file type (AIFF or BWF/.WAV), sample rate, and bit-depth. Clicking OK will bring up the Save As destination window, asking you to name the session and hard drive location for saving.

Note: Saving a new session created from a template does not overwrite the template. Template data, once written, cannot be altered. Deleted yes, altered no. If you come up with a session format that you think you'll be using again, save it as a template using the "Save As Template…" selection from the File menu. This will prompt you to choose a name and location for the new session template, and whether or not any recorded media should be included in the template. (I can't think of a situation in which you would choose to save audio media in a music session template, but for post-production sessions, we will save test tones, 2-pops, and beep series for use in film/TV ADR and mix sessions.)

Building a Session from Scratch

Sometimes it's just easier/faster to build your session from the ground up. If you are using mainly stereo inputs, or if you have complex routing tasks, it may behoove you to create a session from jump street. Use the Shift + Command + N key combination to bring up the New Track dialog, or simply select Track > New…from the main menu. This allows you to choose the number, type, and format of sample-based (audio) or tick-based (MIDI) tracks to add to your session.

Naming Tracks

Please, please, *please* name your tracks something other than "Audio 1" before you record anything, particularly if you are handing your session off to another engineer to edit or mix. It will save you a great deal of time if you can identify a track or clip named "Guitar Solo" rather than "Audio 1-0_157." Just double-click in the Track Name pane of the Track window to bring up the naming dialog. From there you can name the track, add comments, and easily navigate to the previous or next track to continue the naming task.

Recording Live Performances

As in life, the recording process unfolds as a series of events. If you've prepared well for your session, the natural order will appear self-evident. Let's examine the sequence in which recording sessions typically progress.

The Recording Process

- **Basic Tracks:** Capturing live performances to hard drive (or other storage media) using multiple tracks of audio, one for each microphone or sound source.
- **Punch-ins:** If the overall performance of a basic track is good, there still may be minor timing or other performance issues that need to be fixed. This is most easily accomplished by doing a punch-in (or spot record) on the track in question. Example: If a bass part is good except for a wrong note in the chorus, the bass player will replay just that portion of the track by punching-in, or recording a section of short duration, on the original performance track. This is best done when the performer is still set up for the tracking session so you don't have to re-create the equipment settings and energy level of the original performance at a later point in time. Pro Tools gives you a number of options for handling punch-ins easily, which we will explore in greater detail later in this book.
- **Overdubs:** Once your basic tracks are recorded, any new parts/tracks that you record on that song will be known as *overdubs*. This is because you are recording new parts or layers in addition to the existing basic tracks. Some songs will require no overdubbing, some will require many layers of overdubs. Some songs are created entirely by overdubbing one track at a time.
- **Editing:** This is the process of selecting keeper takes, fixing timing or tuning errors, editing the content of the performances you've recorded, and otherwise choosing that which will or will not make it to the final mix of the song.
- **Mixing:** Combining all of the tracks in your recording to make a stereo (or surround) mix, suitable for listening on standard consumer playback systems. This is the step in which you balance volume levels between instruments and vocals to achieve the best-sounding final product.
- **Mastering:** This is the final step in the recording process before distribution, and one in which EQ and compression are applied to your mixes to optimize volume and dynamics and make each song in your project sound like it belongs to the same sonic family as the others. A mastering engineer will also smooth out any fade-ins or fade-outs, remove count-offs or dead air from the beginning or end of mixes, and put songs in their proper order with appropriate space between cuts for a CD or vinyl album release.

Some engineers may choose to skip or combine steps; some projects may not require one step or another; each project is different and has to be considered on its own merits; but these are the basic building blocks of typical multi-track recording sessions. Examine these steps and consider how they might apply to the music you are about to record.

Pro Tools Commands for Recording and Playback

Transport Controls

Pro Tools uses a Transport window in addition to keystrokes to access all transport functions. To bring up the Transport window, simply type Command + 1 on the numeric keypad.

The basic transport controls are, from left to right:

Online: Puts Pro Tools into Sync mode, allowing recording or playback when synchronized to an external time code source.

Return to Zero: Moves the cursor to the beginning of the session. Key command: Return on the main keyboard.

Rewind: Moves the cursor earlier in the timeline when pressed or held. Key command: press "1" on the numeric keypad. Holding the rewind button moves the cursor continuously. Clicking the rewind button once (or more) moves the cursor earlier by time increments depending on the scale you have selected in the main Time Scale window:

- *Bars|Beats—1 bar earlier*
- *Min:Secs—1 second earlier*
- *Time Code—1 frame earlier*
- *Feet+Frames—1 foot earlier*
- *Samples—1 second earlier*

Clicking the Rewind button repeatedly moves the cursor earlier in repeated increments.

Fast Forward: Moves the cursor later in the timeline when pressed or held. Key command: press "2" on the numeric keypad. Holding the Fast Forward button moves the cursor continuously. Clicking the Fast Forward button once (or more) moves the cursor later by time increments dependent on the scale you have selected in the main Time Scale window:

- *Bars|Beats—1 bar later*
- *Min:Secs—1 second later*
- *Time Code—1 frame later*
- *Feet+Frames—1 foot later*
- *Samples—1 second later*

Go to End: Locates the cursor at the end of the last clip in your session. Key command: Option + Return.

Stop: Click the Stop button to stop the transport. Key command: space bar or "0" on the numeric keypad.

Play: Begins playback from the current cursor location. Key command: space bar or "0" on the numeric keypad. See the following section for play modifier commands.

Record: Clicking the Record button arms Pro Tools to record on all record-enabled tracks. Clicking Play begins the recording. Key commands: pressing Command + space bar, F12, or "3" on the numeric keypad will each begin recording immediately.

There are two other indicators in the Transport window: a Track Record Enable Indicator and a Track Input Monitor Indicator. The upper box turns red to indicate if you have at least one track record-enabled. The box will appear gray if no tracks are record-enabled.

The lower box turns green to indicate that at least one track is set to monitor Input Only (regardless of record-enable status), gray if all tracks are set to monitor Auto Input.

Transport Window Menu

The Transport window can show as much or as little information as you desire. Choose from display options by clicking the triangle icon on the right side of the Transport window. You will see a menu listing your display options, including:

Counters

This shows or hides the main and secondary counter displays.

MIDI Controls

This shows or hides the MIDI control section of the transport, which displays click/tempo/meter information, count-off status, and allows you one-click access to toggle four MIDI-related states:

Wait for Note: When this is selected, recording will not begin until Pro Tools senses that a MIDI event has been received. Use this when you want recording to begin at the exact time you begin playing a MIDI instrument or send some other MIDI data.

Metronome: When this mode is selected, Pro Tools will generate a regular rhythmic beat that can trigger internal or external MIDI sounds, creating a click track for use in recording or playback. Note: You must create a click track or instrument track in order to assign a sound-source input/output for the metronome click to be heard. This metronome pulse will correspond to the tempo you have set in the Tempo window or Conductor track. Double-click the Metronome button to open the Click/Countoff Options dialog window used to configure the metronome.

MIDI Merge Mode: When highlighted, any newly recorded MIDI information will be merged and added to any existing MIDI information on that track. When deselected (also called "replace mode"), any newly recorded MIDI information will replace whatever was previously recorded on that track.

Conductor Track: Also called the Tempo Ruler Enable button, this activates the Tempo map as defined in the Tempo ruler of the Edit window. When deselected, Pro Tools reverts to Manual Tempo mode and will ignore the Tempo ruler information. Manual Tempo mode allows you to enter a numeric BPM value in the Tempo field, or tap the desired tempo by tapping the "T" key on your main keyboard.

Display the MIDI Controls window by selecting View > Transport > MIDI Controls, or Command + Click the Expand/Collapse "+" button in the Transport window.

Synchronization

This window displays three buttons:

- **Online:** Puts Pro Tools into Sync mode, allowing recording or playback when synchronized to an external time-code source.
- **Gen MTC:** When active, Pro Tools will generate MIDI Time Code and send the signal out to all connected devices capable of receiving MIDI TC.
- **Gen LTC:** When active, Pro Tools will generate Linear Time Code in the format specified in your session setup.

Minimal

Minimizes the size and content of the Transport window. Unless you have selected the Expanded Transport option, the Transport window will only show the main transport control buttons.

All

This selection expands the transport to show all available Transport Module windows.

Expanded Transport

Expands the Transport window display to add more details to the display, including secondary counter, pre/post-roll settings, and the metronome setting details.

Playback Modes

Right-clicking the Play button brings up a menu of playback options, including:

Half-Speed

Selecting this option immediately initiates half-speed playback from the current cursor location. Key command: Shift + space bar, or Shift + Click on Play button.

Prime for Playback

This command pre-loads audio into the playback buffer in order to initiate immediate playback when the Play button is pressed. It is possible for Pro Tools playback to lag the Playback command a bit, particularly when your session contains a large number of tracks. This command allows you to lock playback to time code more quickly as well. Key command: Option + Click the Play button. The Stop button will light, and the Play button will flash. Initiating the Play command will commence immediate playback.

Loop Play

This command will repeat playback of the selected clip until the transport is stopped. To activate Loop Play, highlight a clip, then right-click the Transport Play button and select Loop. Alternately, press Control + Click the Play button to toggle between normal play and Loop Play modes.

Begin playback by pressing the space bar, pressing "0" on the numeric keypad, or clicking the Play button in the transport. To stop playback, click the Stop button, press the space bar, or press "0" on the numeric keypad.

Dynamic Transport Mode

This command decouples the playback start location from the timeline clip selection, allowing you to begin playback from any point on the timeline without losing your timeline clip or edit selection.

Another playback modifier function is the Timeline Insertion/Play Start Marker Follows Playback command.

This is a long-winded name for the option as to whether or not your cursor locates to the place where you stopped playback or returns to the original starting position on the timeline. The key command is accessed by typing the letter "N" on the keyboard. I use this frequently when editing tracks. Note: It is possible to record over previously recorded or edited clips if this setting is not selected during recording. Hit the Play command twice if you are unsure of the setting.

Recording Modes

Right-clicking the Record button brings up a menu of recording mode options, including:

Normal: The default Pro Tools setting is Normal recording mode; when you use a Record command, you will begin recording at the same time and timeline position at which you commence playback. Prior to recording, you may also designate a range in the timeline in which to record audio. If you define a range, the new recording will occupy only that range. (See Auto Punch.) Pre- and post-roll are available in Normal recording mode, but otherwise Pro Tools cannot begin recording if the track is already playing. Normal recording is nondestructive, meaning that all successive passes on the same clip will be named sequentially, displayed in the Clip list, and saved to disk.

Loop: In this mode, when you define a range in the timeline, you will be able to record multiple nondestructive passes one after another, while the section repeats until you stop the playback. The takes are numbered sequentially and placed into the Clip list. Clips can easily be placed in the timeline to audition takes.

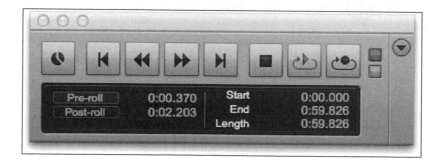

Note: There is an extremely useful variation of this technique when used in conjunction with playlists. In the Preferences menu, click the Operation tab, and check the box marked Automatically Create New Playlists When Loop Recording, under the Record section of the menu. Now when you use Loop Record, you will automatically create a new playlist in the stack for each pass recorded. Auditioning and comping tracks can be managed with ease using this technique.

Destructive: In this mode, you will be permanently deleting and replacing the audio in any clip you happen to record over. While this does save on disk space, the chance of erasing something important is a very real possibility using Destructive recording mode. I would suggest you disable this mode and not ever use it. Disk space is cheap, and performances can be once-in-a-lifetime events. Save everything.

QuickPunch: QuickPunch mode allows you to instantly punch in and out manually during playback anywhere on a record-enabled track. Pro Tools creates a new file from the moment you begin playback, and this clip is stored in the Clip list when you punch in on a track. You may punch in and out up to 200 times in a single pass.

The truly brilliant thing about QuickPunch is that it actually records audio from the point at which you start playback, not just when you hit the Record button. Why is this so great? Let's say that you started playback four bars before the punch, but your manual punch-in was a half second late. With QuickPunch mode, Pro Tools recorded everything from the moment you started rolling. All you have to do is expand the beginning of the new audio clip to reveal the missing half-second. Brilliant! This has saved my bacon innumerable times, particularly when a performer does something really wonderful just before the planned punch-in. When I am rehearsing a performance on a record-enabled track and hear something worth keeping, all I need to do is hit record *before* I stop playback, and Pro Tools has captured the entire take. Love it!

Note: You should consider always using Pro Tools in QuickPunch mode, so that you never miss an opportunity to record a pass.

Disclaimer: Once you stop playback, the QuickPunch buffer is emptied. In order to capture audio or MIDI in QuickPunch mode, you must have assigned a live input source to a record-enabled track *and* hit the record button *before* stopping playback. Additional modes for HD users:

TrackPunch (Pro Tools HD only)**:** With TrackPunch enabled, you can enable/disable record-arming, and punch-in/out on any track or combination of tracks without interrupting recording or playback.

DestructivePunch (Pro Tools HD only): This is a destructive recording mode that allows you to punch in or out on a record-enabled track, thereby replacing the existing audio on the hard drive, and creating a new contiguous file combining new and old audio as recorded on the track.

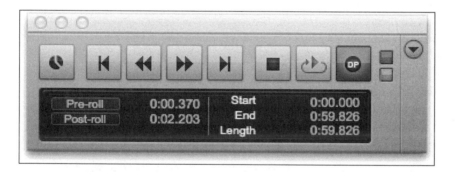

Note: unless you have a specific reason to do otherwise, I would disable this mode and work nondestructively as much as possible. I have worked with Pro Tools for well over a decade and have rarely used any of the destructive recording modes. I'd rather have the option to review and revise edited tracks at a later time.

Using Record Modes

Cycle through each of these modes by Control + Clicking on the Record button in the transport window.

Additional Recording Tools

Auto Punch

When you define a clip in the timeline, you can use an automated punch-in to record in a selected range. Just highlight a range in the Timeline or Edit window of the session, then start recording. The new recording will only occupy the predefined length in the track. You can add pre- or post-roll playback by clicking the appropriate button in the Transport window.

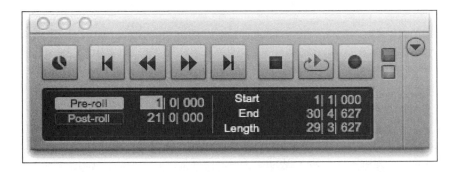

Another Auto Punch technique uses Dynamic Transport: From the Transport window, right-click the Play button, then select Dynamic Transport, or type Command + Control + P. Now define a recording range by dragging the Timeline Selection Start and Timeline Selection End indicators in the main Timebase ruler to encompass the range you wish to record. (Note that these normally blue arrow indicators turn red when a track is record-enabled.)

Then, drag the blue Play Start marker triangle in the same ruler to the point at which you desire playback to begin, effectively using manual pre-roll. (Make sure the Play indicator is located earlier than the start of the recording range.) You can also click in that ruler or use the Rewind or Fast Forward keys to move the Play Start marker. When you click Play, you will audition the recording range with manual pre-roll. When you click Record, you will record that range with pre-roll.

Note: This is unlike QuickPunch, in the sense that Pro Tools does not record audio from the point playback has begun; therefore, you cannot extend the beginning of a recorded clip to reveal pre-roll audio.

Loop Record Mode

In Loop Record mode, you will be able to record multiple passes of audio on successive takes, as the play command continues to cycle recording of the selected clip until stopped. Use this command with the Auto-Playlist option to create a stack of takes on successive playlists.

Double-Tracking

This refers to recording the same part twice, as identically as possible. To add depth to a performance or to create a wider stereo spectrum spread, try double-tracking a part or parts, then panning them opposite one another. This can be done with vocals, background vocals, guitars, horns, or just about anything.

Recording at Half Speed

Little-known fact: with Pro Tools it is possible to record at half-speed, which doubles the speed of the recorded part on normal playback. Click the Record button, then right-click the Play button and select Half-Speed. The track will play back at half speed, and the recording will capture at this speed, thereby doubling the speed at normal playback. Key command: Command + Shift + space bar. Not quite sure how often you would use this trick, since you can easily accomplish the same results by using the Time Compression/Expansion Audio Suite plug-in, but it's fun to find new ways to mess with audio! Google "Les Paul," and listen to his recording of "Lover (When You're Near Me)" for an early example of this technique.

Practical Pro Tools

Recording to a Click—or Not

If you are recording a style of music that requires a constant and unwavering beat, then it makes sense for you to use a click track when recording basic tracks. In addition to working well with MIDI performances, a click track allows you to use the bar/beat boundaries and Grid mode in Pro Tools for precise timing and quantizing parts. This can be very handy when it comes to editing or replacing parts, as the consistent tempo of the original performance will make Cut/Copy/Paste Edit alignment much easier than with constantly varying tempi. Loop-based music, urban, electronic, pop, rock, and country are often cut to a click track.

Music with complex time signature or tempo changes can be programmed in advance, and the basic tracks can then be performed to the custom click track. This type of programming is often employed when recording music for film and TV, or any other visual medium requiring precise synchronization to image.

Some songs simply will not work with a click, and some musicians may find it difficult to play when confined to the inflexible pulse of the metronome. Jazz and classical music may not translate well when performed in time with a click track. As usual, it depends on the song and the musicians performing the piece.

Note: Music that is performed without a click track can still be conformed to a tempo grid after the fact using the Pro Tools Beat Detective function. Likewise, the tempo can be determined after the performance by using the Identify Beat command to create a tempo map.

Creating a Click Track in Pro Tools

The easiest way to create a click track is to select Track > Create Click Track. This creates a new mono Auxiliary track with the DigiRack Click plug-in installed in the Insert pane. From there you may choose different preset click sounds from a drop-down menu in the Click plug-in window, or you may customize a sound based on your needs.

Alternately, you may use the TL Metro plug-in (included in Pro Tools) as a source for your click sound. For more click options, you can install an instrument plug-in (such as Xpand2) on the click track insert, or even choose an external MIDI device by selecting the path of your connected MIDI device in the Track Input selector.

Next, you will need to enable the click track in order to be heard during recording or playback. Via the Options menu, select Options > Click. Alternately, at the top of the Transport window, click the drop-down menu triangle to reveal display options for the MIDI controls and the counters.

Click the Metronome button in the Transport window to activate the click.

Pressing the "7" key on the numeric keypad also toggles the metronome state.

Configuring Click Options
You can quickly enable/disable the click in the Transport window as explained above. In some cases, it can be helpful for performers to hear the click track for a bar or two

before the recording begins, in order to prepare for the passage to be performed and to play in time more accurately. To hear a click countoff before the recording or playback is to begin, click the Countoff button to highlight it. From there, double-click the bar count to select the desired number of bars to countoff before recording or playback.

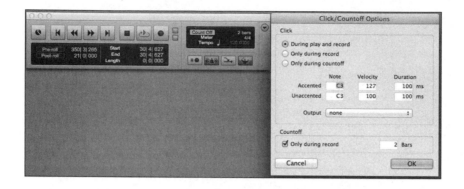

When you need access to more options, you can open the Click/Countoff Options dialog by choosing Setup > Click/Countoff or by double-clicking the Metronome button in the Transport window.

In this window, you can select when you'll hear the click:

- During play and record
- Only during record
- Only during countoff

You can determine the number of bars of countoff, from 1 to 99, and whether you would like the countoff every time you hit play/record or only during recording. This window also gives you access to the MIDI note number, velocity, and duration for both accented and unaccented beats while using an external MIDI source for your click sound. There is a drop-down menu that allows you to choose between connected external MIDI sources.

Note: A click track should usually be used only when the performer or performers are wearing headphones. Playing a click track through speakers will cause it to be picked up by any and every live microphone in the room. If a performer's headphones are fairly loud, the sound of the click may still bleed into nearby mics. To prevent click contamination, always test the click in the headphones to be sure the sound isn't being picked up by adjacent microphones.

Using the Click Track as a Weapon

In nearly every tracking session involving a click track and a drum set, I have found that the drummer will invariably want to hear the click approximately 10 times louder than anyone else in the band. Not a problem if you have the ability to give each musician a customized cue mix, but it can be a tremendous headache (literally) for anyone having to share a mix with the drummer. You can use this lopsided headphone mix to get even with a narcissistic singer, but in the long run, it will wear on the nerves of anyone having to listen to the incessant clacking of the metronome and result in migraine-like symptoms. Not to mention the potential for click leaking from the headphones into the sensitive microphones on the acoustic guitar and piano. The click track can be a mighty production tool...or a formidable weapon. Create at least two discrete cue mixes for your group tracking session if possible, and avoid going to war.

The Headphone Mix

The click track discussion makes a nifty segue into the topic of headphone (or "cue") mixes. Cue mixes are beneficial for tracking musicians, in the sense that they can have a good-sounding mix that allows them to hear exactly what they need to hear to perform to the best of their abilities. The simplest way to build a cue mix is to send the musicians the same main mix that you hear in the control room. This works well for many situations, but when you need to solo or mute a track while musicians are playing during the tracking session, it will affect their mix as well, which may be disorienting or cause them to stop playing. Having a second set of physical outputs on your audio I/O will allow you to create a separate cue mix for the band, freeing you to solo/mute tracks or change the volume levels of tracks in your monitor mix without changing anything in the headphones. The more outputs you have available on your I/O device, the more cue mixes you can create for the performers. Using an 8-channel I/O device gives you the option to have a main stereo mix for the control room and up to three other stereo mixes for the performers. I would suggest using one cue mix for the drummer, one for the singer, and one cue mix for the remaining musicians.

There are headphone mixer systems, such as those from Aviom and Hear Technologies, which allow you to provide discrete mixes for each performer via a mixer that he or she controls. Imagine the time saved and arguments averted by allowing the drummer to crank the click as much as he or she wants without subjecting the rest of the band to that torture! This is also a quick cure for the "more me" syndrome. Suffice it to say that I am a huge fan of individual headphone mixer systems.

Here's how to set up a dedicated cue mix in Pro Tools, assuming you are using an audio I/O device with at least two sets of stereo outputs:

Create a Headphone Aux Send on Each Track: Holding the Option key, click on the Send A pane on the first track in your session (in either the Mix or Edit windows) and select "new track…" In the resulting New Track dialog window, build a stereo Auxiliary Input using Sample Time Base, and name it "Headphones." When you click the Create button, you will have created a headphone mix send in the Send A slot on each track in your session, except for the Master Fader.

Designate a Hardware Output: Locate the headphones' auxiliary sub-master; assign the output to the second (or other desired) set of physical outputs on your audio I/O device. We have already established that the more outputs you have available, the more cue mixes you can create. If you connect multiple audio I/O devices, you can increase the number of cue mixes as well. Note: You will need to use some sort of headphone amplifier, as the output of your I/O is not sufficiently powerful to drive headphones. Only the AVID HD Omni has its own headphone amplifier that can be used to drive headphones.

Set Cue Mix Levels: Click on the Headphones send on any desired track. A small individual Aux send fader will display, allowing you to adjust the level of that particular track in the headphone mix. If you select the Pre button in this window, it becomes a pre-fader send, which maintains the level of that send as set by that fader. The level of this send will not change when the track fader is moved, muted, or soloed. This is the usual operating mode for cue mixes. If you wish the Headphones send level to mirror changes on the track fader level, leave the Pre button unchecked, making this a post-fader send.

You can pan these sends independently of the main mix, or you can have the send pan control linked to the main pan control. To do this, check the FMP (Follow Main Pan) button on the Send page.

Note: holding the Option key when clicking on the FMP or Pre boxes turns it into a global command, applying the change to all tracks/sends.

Copy Main Mix Levels to Cue Mix (For Pro Tools HD only)**:** Select a track by clicking the Track Name field to highlight. Type Command + A to select all tracks. From the top menu, choose Edit > Automation > Copy to Send…, or type Option + Command + H to open the Copy To Send window. Tick the Current Value box in the Copy field, then tick the Volume box in the From field.

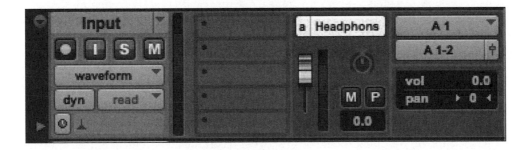

In the To field, select Send A, then click OK. You have now copied all of the main Track fader levels to the Headphones send on every track, which gives your performers the same mix balance you are hearing in the control room. Control overall cue mix level by adjusting the Headphones sub-master fader.

Display Headphones Mix Levels: From here you can make volume adjustments to suit the needs of the performers. To get a visual display of the individual track cue send levels, go to the View menu at the top of the main page, and select View > Sends A–E > Send A. This will display an expanded view of the Send A controls for each track and allows you to easily see the cue mix balance and make adjustments quickly.

Note: A number of these steps have been incorporated into the Record + Mix templates. Big timesaver!

Not all band recording sessions will require a cue mix. I recently tracked a group of bluegrass musicians for whom headphones were a distraction and actually made their performance less confident. They had been accustomed to rehearsing and performing without headphones for years, and found that they could balance and control their own levels much better without them. Solo performers may also choose to record without the benefit of a cue mix. If they are not using headphones, you will still need to find a way to communicate with the performers if you are in the control room and they are in a studio live room. Most studios will have a talkback monitor in the live room for just this purpose. You can send your control room talkback mic signal to the studio monitor speakers in lieu of making the performers wear headphones.

Metering

As you already know, DAW systems record digital audio with a wide dynamic range, especially at 24-bit resolution. It's important to remember that there is a limit to the amount of signal you can effectively record without distorting the signal. This is called full scale, 100 percent modulation, or 0 dB headroom, and the way you know you've hit that ceiling is when the clip indicator (the red light at the top of the meter) is lit. In terms of signal flow, the meter can exist either pre- or post-fader. Pre-fader metering is the default setting in Pro Tools, and it's probably a good idea to leave it that way so you'll know when anything in the signal path on that track is clipping. Yes, a clipped plug-in will glow red as well, but it's much easier to notice the clip indicator on the track meter. Using post-fader metering can lull you into a false sense of security if the fader is pulled down to a lower level, because the clip indicator on the meter may not illuminate even if every plug-in in the chain is clipping. Remember: in digital audio, clipping is *bad*, and you should always avoid it. The meters are set to warn you if just a few consecutive samples are clipped, so if you do encounter some clipping, check the spot on the track that trips the clip indicator light. Solo that spot and listen carefully. If you do not actually *hear* distortion, you're probably okay. Then you must determine if your plug-ins are adding gain to drive level into the red. Manage your gain structure so that you avoid clipping all along the signal path.

Pro Tools employs peak level meters that respond quickly to audio transients. If you are accustomed to setting levels on VU meters, be aware that you do not need to hit the top of the meter in Pro Tools. The equivalent of 0 dB on a VU meter is actually around -14 dB on a peak meter. Pro Tools 11 now comes complete with 4 different metering options. Pro Tools 11 HD comes with 17 metering options. Here, we are using the Pro Tools Classic option.

Setting Levels

It's a good idea to set levels on every microphone before you begin recording. Take the time necessary to listen to every mic on each drum, each vocal, and each instrument individually. This allows you to concentrate on getting your signal path straight and your levels accurately adjusted, and gives you the opportunity to carefully listen to the sound quality of each microphone to be sure you are getting what you really need to hear. We will briefly discuss the selection and placement of microphones later in this book.

If you are recording at 24-bit resolution, then you have plenty of leeway to allow for headroom when setting recording levels. Based on the ballistics of the peak meter as described above, your goal should be to set your recording level at an average of -14 dB with peaks of -6 maximum. Be particularly careful when recording drums, percussion, or any signal with highly transient peaks. Always use your ears to determine if you hear distortion in your recording. While you may have just the right amount of signal from the drum kit when setting levels, remember that a dynamic drummer may give you 6 dB more level when actually recording the song.

The Pro Tools default track size is fairly small; hence, the meter can be too small to read accurately. If you are having a hard time reading the meter, expand the track height by selecting the desired track height from a drop-down list to the immediate left of the track name. Alternately, you can hover the cursor over the bottom edge of the track beneath the track name, then click and drag the edge higher or lower to shrink or expand the track manually. Option + Click on either of these makes the change appear globally. If you claw click (Control + Option + Command) on the meter, it will toggle between normal and wide display, which may make it easier to see and set levels.

Recording with Dynamics Processing

At which point in the recording process do you need to control dynamics: before or after tracking? This is a sticky question, as some engineers prefer to record everything without compression, and some choose to compress every mic they record. Personally, I prefer to record drums, bass, piano, strings, and electric guitar without compression. I will record vocals and acoustic guitar with light compression (no more than -4 dB of gain reduction) in order to control dynamics and avoid digital clipping. Use your ears and your best judgment to find out what works best for you. Just remember that any recorded processing will be there forever; you can't undo compression or other effects on your recorded tracks.

Recording with EQ

If you have selected and positioned your mics carefully, you shouldn't need to equalize very much, if at all, when recording. You may encounter low-frequency rumble with some microphones due to ambient noise, tapping feet, or other artifacts. This can be easily remedied by using a high-pass filter to remove low-frequency information below 60 Hz. Occasionally you may encounter a snare drum with a pronounced peak in the 1 kHz–2kHz range, which can be diminished by using a notch filter or peak EQ tuned to the resonant frequency of the drum. The same axiom applies with equalization as with compression: you can't undo EQ. Be judicious in your use of signal processing on the way into your DAW.

Keeping Track of Tracking Sessions and Files

Use the "Save As…" command to create a new version for every instrument you add or major edit you make to the song. I use a naming convention that starts with the number of the version followed by the name, then the instrument or action, then any iterative numbers. For example, if I have already tracked a song and am about to add a piano overdub, I would name the session "SongName PNO_01." A subsequent version with a second round of piano overdubs might be called "SongName PNO_02." Unless you change the location when saving, all these Pro Tools sequence files will be stored in the session folder on your hard drive. This may seem like an unwieldy format for naming files, but in a list of 10 or more saved sequences, it's always easy for me to find the version I worked on last, or the version with the first vocal overdubs, or the version of SongName that had a corresponding rough mix named "SongNameRoughMix03." Here's a screen shot showing how this would look in a session folder.

Summary of Key Commands

Operation	Key Command
New Session	Command + N
New Track	Shift + Command + N
Transport Window	Command + 1
Go To End	Option + Return
Stop	Space bar, or 0 on the numeric keyboard
Play	Space bar, or 0 on the numeric keyboard
Record	Command + Space bar, F12, or 3 on the numeric keypad
Half-Speed Playback	Shift + Space bar, or Shift + Click Play button
Prime For Playback	Option + Click Play button
Loop Playback	Control + Click Play button to Toggle command
Timeline Insertion/Play Start Marker Follows Playback Command	N
Toggle Record Modes	Control + Click Record button
Dynamic Transport	Command + Control + P
Half-Speed Record	Command + Shift + Space bar
Select All Tracks	Click Track Name pane, then Command + A
Copy To Send	Option + Command + H
Wide Meter Display	Control + Option + Command + Click Meter
Keep Plug-in Window open	Shift + Click plug-in name or Insert button
Copy Plug-in Settings	Shift + Command + C
Paste Plug-in Settings	Shift + Command + V
Copy Plug-in Assignment	Option + Drag plug-in

Chapter 3 Review

1. When should you consider bit rate and sample rate for your sessions?
   a. When buying your Pro Tools system
   b. During pre-production
   c. When building a new Pro Tools session
   d. All of the above
2. True or False: Pro Tools allows you to mix audio files with different bit and sample rates within the same session. _____
3. When creating a new session, you must choose between the following audio file formats for your session: _____ or _____.
4. To commence playback from the current cursor location, click the Play button on the Transport window, or simply press the keyboard _____ or the _____ key on the numeric keypad.
5. The Transport window can show _____ different counter displays.
6. The following MIDI controls can also be accessed from the transport: _____, _____, MIDI Merge mode, and _____, which is also called the Tempo Ruler Enable button.
7. When would you need to put Pro Tools into Online Synchronization mode? Whenever Pro Tools needs to sync to an _____.
8. True or False: Clips erased or recorded using Destructive Record mode can be restored by using the Undo command. _____

9. The key command for initiating half-speed playback is _____ + _____ . You can also Shift + Click on the Play button in the Transport window.
10. Loop Play mode is accessible by right-clicking on the Play button to expose a menu of playback options, or by _____ clicking on the Play button to toggle through the playback modes until Loop mode is reached.
11. Several recording modes are accessible by right-clicking the Record button. These modes are:
    a. _____
    b. _____
    c. _____
    d. _____
    e. _____
    f. _____
    g. _____
12. Loop Record mode creates a new _____ for each recorded audio or MIDI pass.
13. With _____ enabled, new audio and/or MIDI is stored in a buffer from the point at which playback begins.
14. You may use a number of methods to create a click track in Pro Tools. The fastest method is to select the _____ menu > Create Click Track. This creates a new aux track and installs the DigiRack _____ plug-in automatically.
15. Pro Tools displays _____ type meters on every audio and aux track.
16. One of the advantages of recording at 24-bit resolution is the wide _____ range.
17. What hardware is required in order to create a dedicated headphone mix out of Pro Tools? _____
18. Clicking the FMP button on a send fader enables that send to _____ settings.
19. The AVID _____ interface has its own built-in headphone amplifier.
20. The _____ command allows you to store and rename a new version of your session on your session hard drive.

Chapter 4
THE RECORDING PROCESS

Recording a song or a collection of songs can at times be like assembling building blocks; at other times it is very much like assembling a jigsaw puzzle. It's important to understand how the pieces of the recording puzzle fit together, as each step is dependent on the others. Let's take a look at each step in the process of recording music.

Tracking

This is the process of recording one or more new tracks of audio into your recorder or DAW. Typically, the source of these recordings is a live instrumental or vocal performance. Tracking can also refer to recording a MIDI performance as MIDI data or the recording of MIDI tracks into your DAW as audio files. Tracking can involve one musician or many. You can track one musician at a time in successive layers or many musicians at once on multiple tracks.

Editing

Once your tracks have been recorded, they can be modified nondestructively to adjust for accuracy or quality of performance, or to change the arrangement/orchestration. Pro Tools excels at providing all the tools necessary to edit audio and MIDI tracks, adjust timing and pitch, or apply any type of creative processing you can imagine.

Mixing

Mixing is the ultimate combination of multiple recorded tracks into a stereo (or multi-channel) master. This is accomplished by balancing the volume levels of recorded tracks in relation to one another in a pleasing fashion, panned between left and right speaker channels, resulting in a stereo "mix." Mixing is typically the final step in the recording process.

The quality of your final product is directly related to the quality of the work at each stage in the process. I refer to this as the "weakest link" theory. Your mix will only sound as good as the original recording. If your original recording/performance quality is poor, chances are you won't get the greatest results in your mix, no matter how much time you spend editing, fixing, or patching tracks together. It is a commonly held misconception that you should "fix it in the mix." Instead, I would urge you to take the time to create an acoustically accurate and noise-free recording environment, select and position your microphones carefully, and record the best performances you can. If you get it right at each step along the way, there shouldn't be many problems to "fix" in the mix.

Mastering

Also referred to as a type of audio post-production, mastering is the final step in the recording process, during which your mixes are prepared for distribution or duplication. The goal in mastering is to optimize the sound of music mixes for playback on a wide array of sound systems and in a variety of media, ranging from vinyl LP to CD to compressed data file formats.

Recording Tracks That Sound Good

- **Start with a good performance.** According to megaplatinum record producer Keith Olsen: "The best parts are in the phone book." In other words, if a part calls for an expert performance, bring in the best player available to perform the part. Start with quality, and it raises the level of quality for the whole project.
- Let's revisit the weakest link concept again for a moment. A good drummer playing a good set of drums with new heads will record well in a room with good acoustics, even if you use inexpensive mics. But change the drummer or some of the other variables, and you may get very different results.
- In the cases where you must work with a less-than-stellar recording, poor quality instruments, or an inconsistent performance, Pro Tools gives you a number of tools to adjust timing, pitch, and timbre to make the best of the performances you have captured. We will delve into these tools in greater detail later in the book, including practical examples in audio and video for you to explore.
  a. **Pick the right mic for the job, and...**
  b. **Put the mic in the right place.** These are the two most powerful tools in a recording engineer's toolkit. There is enough information on these subjects to fill a number of books, and I encourage you to research microphone technology and miking techniques in order to better understand the challenge. We will discuss mics and placement in a very general manner in this book, but I will endeavor to make suggestions when and where appropriate.
- **Select the appropriate signal chain.** What is a signal chain? It is the path by which your audio travels between the performer, the DAW, and your speakers. It can start with a high-quality microphone (or other transducer) and includes cables, patch bays, microphone pre-amps, signal processors (such as compressors or EQs), and A/D convertors, and ultimately ends up as an audio file in your DAW, playing back through a D/A, amplifier and speakers or headphones. It's not just about selecting a "good" mic or an expensive mic pre, it's about assembling the right combination of components to capture that particular performance in the best possible manner.
- **Record signals at the proper level.** If you get the previous steps right, you will be off to a good start. However, your recording may yet be compromised if you capture signal at levels too low or too high to be usable. Too little amplitude can cause you to raise the level of a signal in the mix, increasing audible noise along with content. Too much signal can cause clipping of analog components and distortion (over modulation) in digital components, including plug-ins. We will discuss the concepts of proper level,

unity gain, noise floor, and distortion later in this book. Note: I'm a huge proponent of learning the rules of audio first, then figuring out when and how to break those rules in order to achieve the desired outcome. Creative use of distortion is a prime example.

- **Once recorded, play back the track to be sure you have what you need and that it sounds good.** Just because the meters move and the lights light up doesn't necessarily mean that you have recorded a useable track. Even if you can see waveforms on your computer screen, always use your ears to determine whether or not something sounds right.

Thinking Like a Tracking Engineer

Engineers must concentrate on the tasks at hand when recording, which means listening for unwanted noise and distortion as well as keeping an eye on the meters at each gain stage in the signal chain and listening for things in the recording that may potentially cause problems in the mix. An experienced engineer can do all these things, in addition to noting section markers, making performance notes, ordering lunch, and entertaining the client's entourage, all at the same time. In a band tracking session, you will have to keep an eye on remaining disk space, computer system resources, and the guitar player's intonation as well. There are myriad details to wrangle in the heat of battle, and we cover a good many of them in the various sections of this book.

Keeping an Eye on the Big Picture

Technical needs aside, a good engineer will also be thinking like a producer. Musicians will often look to the engineer for an objective opinion on a take or on how things are working together in an arrangement.

Delivery Format

Is this for a label CD release? Is it a band demo? Maybe a soundtrack for a video game? You need to know the answer to this question before you start the project. The answer will inform you about sample and bit rate, file format, and delivery standards when completed. It will be useful to keep the end goal of the project in mind as you record more and more tracks. This will help keep everyone focused on the quality of the outcome.

What Makes a Recording Sound Bad?

We've touched on a few things above that can detract from the quality of a recording, ranging from technical issues to performance issues. Still, it is possible to record properly from a technical viewpoint and end up with tracks that do not meet industry standards for quality. This can have to do with things such as noise, phase cancellation, EQ imbalance, or a host of other issues. Even monitoring at levels too high or too low for the listening environment can cause you to hear inaccurately and make faulty decisions based on false perceptions.

Recording is often a game of "weakest link." Here are a few things to add to your pre-session technical checklist to help avoid weak links:

- Be sure that your digital sync (a.k.a., word clock) is connected and adjusted properly. Many digital I/O devices have internal sync, but for those of you using external word clock sync devices, be certain that the device is properly connected and that you have digital sync lock. Improperly connected or uncalibrated word clock sources can cause digital jitter, recording at the wrong speed/sample rate, encoding errors and artifacts, or complete recording failure at worst.

- Using defective instruments, microphones, or processing gear can result in poor-quality recordings. Check your gear carefully before recording begins.
- Woodwind players should use new reeds, if applicable.
- Pianos need to be tuned.
- Check other instruments for intonation, and adjust.
- Keep a good tuner handy.
- Change all guitar and bass strings.
- Put on new drum heads.
- If your equipment uses a replaceable battery, put in a new one.
- Tube amplifiers might need new tubes or rebiasing of old ones.
- General buzzing and RFI noise in your signal may be the result of damaged or old cables.
- Unwanted noise may be introduced by using the wrong cables for the job (e.g., using unshielded speaker cables instead of shielded cables to carry instrument level signal).

Note: guitars with single-coil pickups are notorious for buzzing. This noise can be reduced simply by pointing the guitar in a different direction. While monitoring the guitar input, turn by a few degrees in any direction, then listen to see if the character of the noise has changed. If it's louder, turn the other direction until it gets quieter or goes away. If the noise does not go away, you may need to check your cable for breakage, or lift the ground on your amplifier or other signal processor.

Your environment can be a potential source of problems in recording as well.

- Studio acoustics have a great deal to do with the sound of the instrument or voice to be recorded. Recording in a small room with nearly square dimensions can result in a recording that has audible overtones. There are a good many books and articles out there relating to studio acoustics. Start reading!
- Be aware of exterior or interior noises. An adjacent washing machine or nearby jackhammer crew can make uninvited guest appearances on your recording if you're not careful. When in doubt about background noise, listen through headphones to see if there's anything present that may haunt you later.
- If your AC power source fluctuates, or if your recording system is on the same circuit as a refrigerator or high current electric motor, you may encounter serious noise problems.
- Lighting dimmers can cause hum in a signal chain as well as high-impedance signal-carrying cables.
- If your mic cables run directly alongside AC cables, you may experience hum or noise.

Note: audio signal cables should cross AC cables at a 90-degree angle, not run alongside. If signal and AC cable runs must be parallel, keep them at least 12 inches apart to avoid inducing hum.

If you prepare your recording environment effectively, calibrate your recording equipment, and calibrate your ears before you begin, you will eliminate most of the variables that can lead to bad recordings. Which leaves operator error, pretty much.

There are numerous examples of accidental sounds making their way onto recordings. One particular case involves the Led Zeppelin song "Since I've Been Loving You." Listen to the album version of this song, if you have access to it; you'll only need the first 30 seconds. If you have good speakers or headphones you will hear, in between kick drum beats, the sound of a very squeaky kick drum pedal. Now it doesn't ruin the song, because it's a great performance. However, it should provide you with two important lessons:

- Always check your instruments for squeaks or other noises before you record them.
- Always keep a can of WD40 handy.

Calibrating Your Ears

Critical listening is a key component of preparing for any session. You calibrate your gear, why not your ears as well?

A good way to train your ear is by listening for specific components within an existing mix. For example: Take a familiar song and listen, concentrating only on the drums. Try to ascertain how the engineer and producer got them to sound that way. In many cases, that information can be found online in interviews with the production team. If the drums sound like they are being played in a gymnasium, try to find out if they actually were, or perhaps the mix engineer just used a large-hall reverb sound in the mix. Does the kick drum have a lot of high-end as well as low-end frequency information? How did it get that way? Was it due to the sound of the drum, or the mic selection, or was it EQed that way during the mix? Even if you can't come up with a definitive answer, the exercise will help you learn to isolate and listen to one component in the middle of a complex mix surrounded by lots of other instruments and vocals. Once you train your ears and your brain to concentrate on the individual components of a mix, you can mentally pull apart any mix and begin to draw conclusions about how those sounds were achieved. This critical listening/analysis process forms the basis for experimentation and emulation, which will give you additional tools for your engineer toolkit.

Basic Tracking Tools

Let's review the basic components necessary to record live performances in your DAW.

Microphones

There are different flavors of microphones, seemingly one for every kind of recording you might encounter. A microphone is a transducer that uses some form of thin material (paper, plastic, or metal) suspended in a magnetic field, vibrating in response to the pressure of sound waves, thereby turning acoustical energy into electrical energy. Here are some of the common types of microphones:

Condenser Microphones

These mics use a very thin diaphragm made of plastic or metal, and require a battery or an external power source (such as 48 volt, or phantom power) in order to create the electromagnetic field in which the diaphragm is suspended. There is some amplification of signal as well, providing a higher output and wider dynamic range than other types of microphones. Condenser mics typically have a wider range of frequency response as well and are more sensitive to low-amplitude signal. Large-diaphragm condenser mics generally use a diaphragm element with a diameter > 1 inch, while small-diaphragm condensers employ a diaphragm < 1 inch in diameter.

Large-diaphragm condensers are good for vocals, piano, drum overheads—just about anything that generates a wide range of frequencies or requires extended low-frequency sensitivity.

Small-diaphragm condensers are good for acoustic guitar, piano, strings—anything that should be recorded with nearly flat-frequency response.

Tube Microphones

A tube microphone is a type of condenser mic that uses vacuum tubes and a high-voltage external power supply to create the magnetic field and amplification necessary for operation. Tube mics often have a more identifiable "sound" than condenser mics, due to the tube signal amplification, which results in increased low- to mid-range sensitivity and a small amount of pleasing harmonics distortion. Tube mics tend to be more delicate and more expensive than other microphones.

Tube mics are great for vocals or any instrument that does not demand instantaneous transient peak response.

Note: you do not need to use phantom power with tube microphones. They have their own power supply.

Dynamic Microphones

A dynamic microphone uses a permanent ceramic or metal magnet in conjunction with a suspended diaphragm to turn sound waves into audio signal. A dynamic mic does not require a power source. These mics are much simpler than condensers and are more robust and sturdy, as a rule. They are also likely to have a tailored frequency response, while condensers tend to be more flat.

Dynamics are great for drums, bass, guitar amps, some voices, and anything that requires directivity and resistance to high SPL.

Ribbon Microphones

Ribbon mics are dynamic mics that use a small aluminum ribbon suspended between the poles of a permanent magnet. These mics are prized for their smooth high-frequency response and detail (as compared with condensers). Most ribbon mics are high impedance, which means that you should select your mic pre-amp carefully in order to make the most of the meager signal.

Ribbon mics can sound great on voice, horns, guitar amps—anything that benefits from controlled high-frequency response.

Note: *Do not* use phantom power with a ribbon microphone! (Unless the manufacturer specifies otherwise, as in the Royer R122.) The ribbon diaphragm element is very sensitive and will be damaged when you apply phantom power. Most microphone pre-amps give you the option to turn phantom power on/off, but some mixers have a global switch that enables phantom power on all channels. Beware!

Boundary Microphones

Boundary mics use a small condenser mic-head facing a metal plate (or boundary) from a few thousandths of an inch away. Because of their unique design, boundary mics have a hemispherical pickup pattern and almost no physical handling noise. These mics are relatively flat in both appearance and frequency response and are useful for room mics, under-lid piano mics, or on a stage floor to capture tap-dancing or dialog close to the floor.

Crystal Microphones

Crystal mics use a diaphragm connected to a crystal element to produce a high-impedance signal. These mics have limited frequency response but are fairly robust. While they were initially used for PA announcements, these mics are now greatly prized by harmonica players. Often played through a small, overdriven tube amplifier, this is the distinctive sound of the blues harp we all know and love.

Direct Boxes

The direct box, or DI (short for Direct Input, or Direct Injection), is a device for converting unbalanced high-impedance signal into balanced low-impedance signal for recording or PA use. A passive DI can use a simple impedance transformer for conversion, while battery- or phantom-powered active direct boxes convert impedance, amplify signal, and may offer options to reverse audio polarity, lift signal ground, or attenuate input. DIs are frequently used when recording bass, guitar, or keyboards without an external amplifier. A DI will also balance your signal, allowing for longer cable runs and better noise rejection.

Signal Chain

Microphone Pre-Amplifiers

A microphone pre-amplifier, or mic pre, is a device that takes low-level input from a microphone (0–100 microvolts) and amplifies the signal to a level sufficient for processing with a recording device (0–10 volts). That's the clinical description; in practice, the selection of a mic pre can have as much impact on the recorded sound as the selection and placement of a microphone. Many studios will have a variety of mic pre's from which to choose, ranging from very clean and transparent sounding hi-fidelity transistor models to tube-mic pre's having very definite sound quality and character.

Compressor/Limiters

A compressor/limiter is an electronic device used for dynamic amplitude range control. Think of it as an automatic gain control that responds to the amplitude of the input signal. You can set a compressor/limiter to automatically reduce the output level by a predetermined amount based on an input-level threshold setting. Any increase in level above this threshold will result in a reduction of gain at the output of the device. The amount of gain reduction is determined by the compression ratio selected by the user. We'll delve into compression later in the book, but for now, think of it as an automatic means to control dynamic range and avoid overmodulation when recording.

Equalizers

EQ, or equalization, is the process of increasing or decreasing the amplitude of a band of frequencies. An equalizer is an electronic device designed to give you amplitude control of narrow frequency bands. In general terms, an EQ allows you to make the high, middle, or low frequencies of your signal louder or softer. There are different types of EQs:

Shelf EQ

A high-frequency shelf equalizer increases or decreases energy at and above the set frequency. A low-frequency shelf equalizer increases or decreases energy at and below the set frequency.

Parametric EQ

Gives you the ability to select a frequency center point (or peak), vary the bandwidth (or Q) of the frequencies near the center point, and make them louder or softer. Multi-band parametrics can be very powerful tools when combined to make notch filters.

Quasi-Parametric EQ

Pretty much like the parametric but without the Q control. Used on many mid- and lower-priced mixing consoles.

Graphic EQ

Separates the frequency spectrum into fixed bands (typically 31, or 1/3 octave), each with its own level control, which can then be made louder or softer independent of adjacent frequencies.

British-Style EQ

Made popular on British recording consoles, this is a combination of four equalization types in a single channel, typically:

- High Shelf
- Upper mid peak
- Lower mid peak
- Low shelf

EQ types also include notch filters, bandpass filters, high-pass filters, and low-pass filters.

DAW

The DAW, or Digital Audio Workstation, is an electronic device for use as an audio recorder, editor, and playback system. In the world of Pro Tools, DAW refers to your computer, Pro Tools software, and the audio I/O interface attached to it.

I/O

The I/O is an audio input/output device, typically housing audio inputs and outputs with A to D and D to A convertors and a means by which to connect to a computer. This can be a USB, FireWire, or other proprietary interface.

Monitor Speakers

Monitoring your recording is a critically important part of the process: if you cannot listen accurately, you will not record accurately. You may not hear buzzes or noises that could ruin a good performance, or you may not get a clear picture of the frequency content of your source for the recording. Your speakers should be a matched pair, should be capable of reproducing low and high frequencies equally well, and should have sufficient power to play back at peaks of up to 95 dB SPL without clipping.

It's best if you alternate listening between at least two pairs of speakers (near-field vs. mid-field) to check your tracks. This helps you avoids listening fatigue and provides a different perspective on various frequencies. Try listening at different levels to hear what stands out at low volume vs. high volume. Use an amplifier that matches the specification of each speaker you will be using (if applicable).

It is common to use powered monitors that are self-contained, meaning that they have built-in amplification and crossover electronics.

Near-Field Monitors

This type of speaker is typically what you might find attached to the average home stereo (if there is such a thing anymore). Near-fields are fairly compact "bookshelf" speakers that are capable of delivering 85–95 dB with little distortion or coloration. Near-fields are best for referencing vocals during recording, as they are the most representative of real-world playback.

Mid-Field Monitors

These are larger speakers that can deliver higher volume and wider frequency response. Mid-field speakers are great for checking the low-frequency content of the kick drum and bass guitar.

Headphones

For engineers, another way to check the fine details of your tracks is to monitor on a good set of headphones. You'll be able to hear very distinctly many things you'd never pick out on speakers, such as noisy microphone cables, talking in the background, squeaky kick drum pedals—all kinds of things. Don't monitor exclusively on headphones, but do use them to occasionally check your tracks.

Headphone Mixes for Performers

Whether using a general mix or offering a custom mix per musician, you will usually need some method of generating a headphone mix for each musician in the studio during the recording. If your I/O device has more than two audio outputs, you can use the additional outs to create a dedicated headphone mix. This can be handy when tracking, as building a separate mix just for the musicians will allow you to solo instruments and vary mix balances in the control room without affecting the musicians' headphone mix. (Changing the musicians' mix in the middle of a take can be disorienting and may cause them to stop playing, potentially ruining a good take.)

It is not unusual for a group of musicians to decline headphones if they are accustomed to performing at once. I recently recorded a bluegrass group whose members had never used headphones in the studio...until the second song of the session. The result? Their playing style changed completely, and it took a good hour to get them a mix they felt they could work with. Still, the quality of the performance was not up to their first take sans headphones, so we abandoned the whole headphone idea. The results were much more pleasing and musical.

Effects Used in Tracking

Analog Processing

It is common practice to use analog compression or EQ on an input source when recording. This happens in the physical world, before signal reaches your I/O device. A typical signal chain would be:

- Microphone
- Mic pre
- Compressor
- EQ
- DAW I/O

These devices would be connected in sequence, using cables and/or a patch bay for connection.

Note: Be careful not to overuse these effects, because once they are recorded, there is no undo function. An overcompressed performance will remain so, and an over-EQed track cannot be un-EQed.

Digital Effects

Because of the *latency* (delay) inherent in using effect plug-ins, I advocate for using as few effects as possible during a tracking session. Latency affects timing, and performing an overdub to match a track that has a plug-in-induced delay can cause all kinds of timing headaches down the road when editing/mixing. Patching a reverb on an Aux send/return bus is an acceptable method of introducing effects on a tracking session. You can use this method with delay or other effects as well.

Avoid inserting plug-ins on tracks that are record-enabled to avoid timing issues. If you *must* insert an EQ or compressor plug-in, try to use the most time-economical version available. The stock DIGI compressor and EQ plug-ins employ a very short delay, somewhere in the 2–10 sample delay realm. Host-based processor DAWs use more computer resources than DSP-based HDX systems, thereby introducing more delay. If you're using anything short of an HDX system, you should keep tracking plug-ins to a minimum.

Note: Do not use delay compensation when tracking or overdubbing! ADC (Automatic Delay Compensation) works by calculating the longest plug-in delay in the session, then delaying *all* tracks to match that amount. This will create monitoring and timing problems for the performing musicians, as they will hear their performance later than real-time by up to a half-second.

Chapter 4 Review

1. The process of recording one or more tracks into your DAW is called _____.

2. A microphone is a type of _____.

3. Condenser microphones require an external power source. Tube mics use a dedicated power supply, while other condensers use an external 48v source known as _____.

4. True or False: Ribbon microphones should always be used with a phantom power source. _____

5. The abbreviation DI is short for _____ or _____.

6. A _____ is used to amplify microphone signal to a level sufficient for use in recording.

7. A _____ is an electronic device used for controlling dynamic amplitude range.

8. An EQ is a tool for modifying _____ content.

9. A notch filter can be created using a _____ equalizer.

10. The abbreviation DAW stands for _____.

11. An _____ is the device used to send and receive audio to and from a computer.

12. It is advisable to monitor your work on a variety of speaker systems, including _____, _____ , and headphones.

13. True or False: Applying signal processing to an audio recording can be reversed in your DAW at a later time. _____

14. The term _____ refers to any compression, EQ, or other processing used between a microphone and a DAW.

15. Inserting a plug-in on a record-enabled track introduces a delay called _____.

16. ADC is an acronym that stands for _____.

Chapter 5

RECORDING IN PRO TOOLS

Recording Instruments

As discussed in the previous chapter, recording engineers have two critical choices to make when recording live instruments: *selecting the right microphone and putting that microphone in the right place*. In this chapter, we will break down the miking process one instrument at a time. The techniques listed here are suggestions to get you started.

Drums

It's not always about the drums. Except in rock music. Or country, hip hop, electronic, pop, jazz, and some classical tunes. So let's get the drums recorded right, and the rest of our project will go much more smoothly.

While some classic records feature drums recorded with one or two microphones for the entire kit, I'm going to suggest that you use no less than eight for a standard drum kit consisting of a kick, snare, three toms, plus cymbals. You can always mute tracks to get back to the old-school sound. Here's the basic layout:

Kick: For a more aggressive sound, use a large-diaphragm dynamic mic inside the drum pointed at the beater. For a better-rounded tone, use a large-diaphragm condenser mic outside the drum pointed at the front head, or on the beater side facing the head.

Snare: A small-diaphragm dynamic mic at a 45-degree angle to the top head looking toward the center of the drum will provide a great overview of the sonic information coming from the top head of the snare drum. You can supplement this with a small-diaphragm condenser mic on the bottom head to add more of the high-end snap of the snare strainer. If you do use two mics, experience dictates that you be prepared to flip phase on one of the snare mics. This can be done in post with an EQ plug-in.

Hi-Hat: A small-diaphragm condenser mic positioned 4 inches above the outside edge of the hi-hat will give you a full-range picture of the hats. The position of the mic is critical here, in that the mic should not see the snare drum if possible. The snare is so loud that it may obscure the hi-hat on its own microphone.

Tom-Toms: Dynamic mics work well if the drummer plays hard. If the parts are more subtle, you can try small- or large-diaphragm condensers. Remember that you will need to keep them a bit further from the drum heads, and those mics will pick up the rest of the drum kit. It's a delicate dance, but with a little practice, you'll find the right combination for your recording.

Overheads: A spaced pair of large-diaphragm condensers or an X-Y pair of small diaphragm condensers will do nicely. If you want to try something a little more exotic, use a pair of PZMs (boundary mics) mounted on the wall on either side of the kit to get a roomier sound from your overheads.

Room Mics: If you have the capacity to record the extra tracks, I strongly advise that you record a stereo pair of room mics. Usually small- or large-diaphragm condensers will work well for this purpose. You can add these tracks in the mix to create a small amount of ambience or a huge amount of garage to the sound.

If you select and position your mics properly, there should be little need for compression or EQ during the recording.

Naturally, each mic gets its own track in the Pro Tools session. You should create a group assignment for all of the drum mics so that they can be muted or level-adjusted as a group. Highlight the track names of all drum tracks, and type Command + G to bring up the Create Group dialog. Label the group "DRUMS" and click OK to create the group.

Electric Bass

Use a direct box to interface the output of the bass with your mic pre-amp, and close-mic the speaker of the bass amp if applicable. The bass amp will typically provide a more aggressive, slightly distorted sound than the DI. You should be able to adjust between the two during mixdown to achieve a good balance of transparent direct sound and the grit of the bass amp.

Observe headroom carefully on your bass tracks. Dynamic range control might be advisable if the bass player is using slapping/popping techniques. The resulting transients can very easily send a track into clipping.

Acoustic Bass

An acoustic bass generates a lot of sound. Because of its size, the sound comes from all over the instrument, making it hard to capture accurately with just one microphone. If you need to record with one mic, select a large-diaphragm condenser and place it about 4 to 6 inches above the bridge.

With two mics, use a large-diaphragm condenser mic 4 inches away from the treble F-hole, and a ribbon mic aligned with the fingerboard and positioned 4 to 6 inches above the strings at the octave.

My preferred method is to use two mics plus a D/I. If a bass player has a pickup installed, it's usually a contact pickup affixed to the bridge. This will provide mid-range frequency content, plus more of the transient attack derived from plucking the strings near the bridge. These three tracks can be mixed together to deliver the best and most realistic sound from the bass.

Electric Guitar

The range of tones available from an electric guitar/amplifier can be very broad, encompassing everything from super clean and bright country sounds to blazing heavy metal distortion and everything in between. Nowadays, most guitar players have evolved their own signature sounds and rely on an array of processing pedals (stomp boxes and other outboard processors) to add effects to create those sounds. This is an instance in which it is preferable to record an instrument with signal processing on the track. If there is any question about whether or not to record with a particular effect—flanging, for example—record without the effect, then add it in the mix.

When recording a guitar amp, you have many choices for microphone selection and placement, and just about anything goes if it sounds good in the track. The basic two-mic setup is a dynamic (or ribbon) mic close to the speaker cone and a large-diaphragm condenser mic four feet away from the speaker cabinet. Though the tracks can be panned hard-left and hard-right, this is not really a *stereo* miking technique, so record each of these mics on its own track. That gives you the option to process, pan, and mix these tracks independently.

Acoustic Guitar

The function of the acoustic guitar in a song will determine how it should be recorded. If it's playing a strummed rhythm part, use a small diaphragm condenser positioned near the 15th fret. A finger-picked part or melody line should be miked nearer the sound hole, preferably on the treble side of the instrument.

Piano

There are three basic techniques I use for stereo-miking a piano:

Close Miking: Using a matched pair of large-diaphragm condenser mics, position them four inches above the hammers and about two feet apart. Lid may be open or closed. Good for rock, pop, and country recordings.

Mid-Distance Miking: Using an X/Y stereo bar, mount a pair of small- or large-diaphragm condenser mics in an X/Y configuration at the bend in the piano (lid open), approximately a foot above the rim of the piano, parallel to the floor, and pointing into the open piano lid. Great for jazz, solo piano, and classical recordings.

Distance Miking: Using a pair of large-diaphragm condenser mics, you can utilize a spaced-pair, Blumlein, or X/Y stereo configuration. This technique requires a large, good-sounding room free from external noises. This is a useful solo or classical miking technique.

Organ

Assuming you have a Leslie cabinet attached to your organ, use a stereo pair of small-diaphragm condenser mics on the upper rotating horn and a single large-diaphragm condenser mic on the lower drum.

Keyboards

Use two active D/I boxes when possible. When miking an amplifier or speaker cabinet, use a dynamic close-mic on a single speaker or two mics on a stereo amp.

Percussion

A stereo pair of small-diaphragm condenser mics positioned as overheads in an X/Y or spaced-pair configuration will pick up a wide range of hand percussion, conga, bongos, and timbales. If you're just miking conga or similar instruments, close-mic them as you would toms on a drum kit.

Other Stringed Instruments

Violin, Viola: Use small-diaphragm condenser mics above and pointing at the faces of the instruments.

Cello: A large-diaphragm condenser mic pointed at the F-hole.

Mandolin, Dobro, Banjo, Ukulele, Oud, Shamisen, Balalaika, and Diddley Bow: Usually a single small-diaphragm condenser mic pointed in the general direction of the sound hole, resonator, or other source of the widest range of frequencies will be the best bet.

Brass Instruments

If you are recording solo brass, try a large-diaphragm condenser mic at a distance of one to two feet. In a group, you can still use individual condenser mics, but you may have better luck with dynamics at a closer range. Be aware that you may need a pop-filter. If you're recording in a large room, use a pair of stereo room-mics.

Wind Instruments

If you are recording solo woodwinds, use a small-diaphragm condenser mic at a distance of one to two feet and pointed at the middle of the horn. You might have success using a second small-diaphragm condenser mic at a distance of four to eight feet from the instrument. In a group, lessen the distance from mic to instrument. If you're recording in a large room, use a pair of stereo room mics here as well.

Recording Unfamiliar Instruments

Position the performer in an open area of your recording space, then walk around the instrument as it's being played. If it's louder than a piano, try a dynamic microphone. If it's quieter, use a condenser mic. Aim for the source of the widest range of frequencies.

As with any of these suggestions, use your ears to determine the best mic selection and placement to capture the best sound. When in doubt, try to make the recorded sound of the instrument match as closely as possible the sound you heard in the room.

Advanced Techniques

Re-Amping

Take an existing recorded track and run it through a secondary process, such as an amplifier emulator plug-in, to add another texture to your sound. You can also use an additional Pro Tools I/O output to send the signal to a guitar amplifier, Leslie rotating speaker, or other external signal processor, then set up a mic and re-record that sound to a new track into your sequence.

This technique is not limited to guitars; you can use this with vocals, drums, or anything, really. Get creative!

Using Multiple Tracks for Guitars

Not to be confused with re-amping, use the double-tracking technique discussed earlier to beef up guitar parts. Then try playing an electric guitar part exactly the same but on an acoustic guitar. Try playing a heavily distorted guitar part using a clean sound, or a different guitar or amplifier, or through a wah pedal depressed halfway. Use half-speed recording mode to give your tracks an otherworldly sound you can't get any other way. Anything goes; this is your opportunity to evolve your own palette of sounds and techniques.

Using a Tuner in Pro Tools

If you are running Pro Tools HD and have installed an AAX DSP instrument tuner plug-in on a track, you can use it in real-time on any available insert slot. Pro Tools HD comes with the TL InTune or BF Essential tuner plug-ins, which give you a variety of display and resolution options. If you are running a host-based system, the process is essentially the same, except you will be using the AAX Native version of the plug-in as opposed to the TDM version of the plug.

Note: The process is a bit more complicated if you are running an HD system and want to use a native-based tuner (or other AAX Native plug-in). Since you cannot have a native plug-in as the only active plug-in on a channel that is record-enabled or in input monitor mode, you have two options:

1. You can use the tuner plug-in on an Aux bus and route instruments to that bus for tuning.

2. There is an advantage in this method, in that using the tuner as an Aux bus plug-in does not negatively impact latency on the input track. This is key to accuracy in timing when performing a live overdub.

3. You can insert any DSP plug-in on an insert before the native plug-in, and it will work. Even if the DSP plug-in is bypassed. Not inactive, just bypassed. Try something small and efficient, such as a Trim plug-in, which will use fewer system resources. Yes, I know, this is crazy, but it works. (It has to do with DSP bus priority and will utilize additional voices.) I can imagine a scenario in which this would be useful, but #1 will always be preferable, IMHO.

Hitting the Red Button

Okay, You've miked every instrument, patched in all your mic pre's and compressors, set your levels, and assigned everything to its proper place in your Pro Tools rig. Now it's time to record something. If you're working with a group of musicians, there's a good chance that they will want to rehearse a song once or twice (or for 12 hours) in order to get acclimated to the headphone mix and be sure they are hearing everything correctly. If they work with a click track, they will be adjusting the level and perhaps the tempo until it's just right. Don't overlook the opportunity to record these rehearsal takes. You never know when someone will play the golden solo or hit something exactly right. Especially when they think it's just a practice pass. When the pressure is off, people tend to play more openly. My advice: hard disk space is cheap; record everything.

Begin recording by clicking the Record button on the Transport, typing Command + space bar, the F12 key, or the number "3" on the numeric keypad. Stop recording by pressing the space bar or the number "0" on the numeric keypad.

If you are recording more than one song in a project, consider saving each song to its own Pro Tools session. This will make it easier to find and audition multiple takes of the same song.

Recording Vocals

Capturing a great vocal performance can be an exhilarating experience or an exercise in frustration. This is an instance in which preparation can truly make a difference and result in a positive experience for all parties. Consider that this session is about more than just gear; it may be about the singer's health, physical ability, preparation, and attitude, as much as it is about your signal flow. The vocal session may be one of the most physically and emotionally demanding parts of a recording project. It can also be one the most rewarding.

Creating a Welcoming Creative Environment

It might seem like an obvious concept, but having the Pro Tools session built, the mic and signal path wired and tested, and the headphone mix up and running will go a long way toward making your singers (or other performers) feel like they are well cared for. If you are ready to rock when they walk in the door, you will earn more brownie points than by making them wait for half an hour while you suss out the buzz in the headphone system. I'm just sayin'.

If a singer is more comfortable singing in his living room, create that vibe by bringing in a comfy chair, a Persian rug, and some candles. If she thrives on playing in bars, turn the lights down low and hang Xmas lights around the room. I once had a singer who was an amazing club performer but nearly shut down entirely in the studio. She needed that club vibe to get comfy. What did we do? Set up tables around the live room and have the band sit at the tables. Then I put up a hand-held mic just under the expensive tube mic and had the singer hang onto it as she would have on stage. The pièce de résistance? She dangled an unlit cigarette from her lip. Voilà! She was transformed into the snarling, prowling stage denizen we hoped she would conjure for the performance. One pass, and done. The moral: do whatever it takes to get the take. (Subject to the laws of the realm and/or commonly accepted social behavior among consenting adults.)

Mic Selection

Every singer has his or her own sound, one reason why there are so many microphones on the market. If you only have one mic, use a large-diaphragm condenser mic with a pop-filter, positioned slightly above and about 6 to 10 inches away from the singer's mouth. Extra points if you have a tube or ribbon mic; now you can test a couple of different microphones to see which is best suited for the vocalist. Set up three (or more) mics, and record the singer singing a verse and chorus of the song in question. On playback, you should be able to jointly determine which mic sounds better. Experiment with distance from the mic and its angle of inclination toward the singer. Always use a pop-filter. If you end up recording a punk singer who insists on using a hand-held mic, put a foam pop-filter on the mic first. It's much easier to eliminate pops and sibilance by taking a preventative approach rather than trying to "fix it in the mix."

Headphones and the Art of Singing in Tune

The right headphone mix can be a blessing, especially with vocalists. But did you know that having your headphone volume cranked can affect your perception of pitch? That's right: the louder the cans, the more your pitch perception is skewed. In particular, the higher frequencies will sound sharper and the lower frequencies will sound flatter, so relying entirely on a pair of closed phones for accurate pitch reference can be dicey. There are three fairly common solutions to this problem:

1. Turn it down!
2. Use semi-open headphones. See AKG and Sennheiser, for example.
3. Take off one ear cup. Just rotate an ear cup toward the back of your head until that ear is free.

If you are able to hear yourself acoustically in the room, your pitch will be much more stable and true.

Vocalist Signal Chain

If you've settled on a suitable mic, the next step is to select a microphone pre-amplifier that will complement the mic and the singer's voice. This is based very much on personal preference, and I will not debate that in this forum. Instead, I will describe in general terms some options and leave it to you to determine what sounds best to your ears.

Mic pre's come in many flavors, but mainly those that are transparent and those that have a signature "sound." The latter can be really cool, if that's the sound you're after. Just remember that once you record a performance, you can't undo that "sound." My preference is usually toward a tube mic pre/channel strip such as the Avalon 737sp. It can be clean if you set it up that way, or it can impart a very distinctive tonal color to the signal.

Compression is often used in recording vocals, but sparingly. Knocking a dB or two off of the peaks is a fine thing, but leave the heavy compression for the mixdown, when you can exercise more precise control.

EQ. This is usually reserved for fixing signal problems on the way in, such as rolling off the low end with a high-pass filter to avoid foot stomping noise and diminish popped p's and such.

If your vocalist has a broadly dynamic style (from a whisper to a scream), it may be useful to split the microphone signal into two mic preamps. Set one for optimum level during the quieter passages (0dB), set the other for optimum level during the loud passages (-12 to -15dB). Record each microphone to its own track in Pro Tools. This gives you the ability to capture vocals having a wide dynamic range without risking distortion.

Vocalist Headphone Mix

Most singers like to hear their voices a few dB above the track, more than you would feel comfortable with in a normal mix. If you can't give them a mixer to create their own mix, then give them a custom mix that meets their needs. (See the earlier section on "The Headphone Mix.")

Add a small amount of reverb to their mix so the vocal doesn't seem so exposed. On an Aux send, use a reverb plug-in that doesn't use a lot of signal processing power, such as D-Verb. Sample the presets to see if you can find one that suits the song. My default D-Verb setting on vocals is as follows:

-2 dB input level, 100 percent wet mix
Room 1, Large
87 percent diffusion
Seconds decay time
0 ms pre-delay
6 kHz HF Cut
No LPF
Be sure to enable Solo Safe mode: Command + Click the Solo button on the Aux track to keep the reverb return from being muted when you solo other tracks.

This will give you a starting point for a basic reverb sound. If you're working on a ballad, you may want to use a hall setting with a longer decay rather than a room setting.

Keeping Track of Vocal Takes and Keepers

Have a lyric sheet handy on which to pencil in notes on each take. Many top-level producers keep an Excel spreadsheet with check boxes per line of lyric so they can rate performances as they happen. I am somewhere in the middle, using a lyric sheet and a legal pad, and I will take notes on the legal pad as the singer performs. (Some things are still better analog.) Occasionally the takes come at you very quickly, and it may make sense to do the vocal comp edit on the fly. Figure out the best system for your work flow. Remember to save a new version before you commence editing takes.

Assembling and Editing Vocal Takes

Refer to the section on comping with playlists.

Double-Tracking

Double-tracking, or *doubling*, is simply recording the same vocal part twice in unison with oneself. This technique became popular in the '50s, as used on records by the greats Les Paul and Buddy Holly. This is sometimes referred to as manual double-tracking.

Automatic Double-Tracking, or ADT, is an electronic means of simulating the slightly random variations of recording a performance twice. Ken Townsend was the Beatles' engineer in 1966, and he developed this technique at the request of John

Lennon. If you listen closely to early Beatles records, you will hear Lennon and McCartney doubling themselves manually. From *Revolver* on, you hear the ADT process in most cases. ADT can be easily achieved after the fact using Pro Tools delay or chorus plug-in effects.

There are differences between and advantages to both techniques, so practice using both.

Using Multiple Tracks for Lead Vocals

Another technique for creating a more dramatic lead vocal sound involves duplicating a vocal part on two or more tracks, then processing them differently.

Use two vocal tracks, panning them opposite each other. Delay one track by 10 to 35 ms. This creates the illusion of 3D space, also called the Haas Effect.

Use two or more vocal tracks. EQ the tracks differently, or modulate the pan setting of one track back and forth between the speakers, or flange one track, or all of the above at once. Use your imagination, this is your sandbox!

Self-Stacking BGVs

If you have a singer capable of doubling his or her existing tracks, it's easy to move to the next step—recording background vocals (BGV) by self-stacking parts. Once the lead vocals are recorded and edited, the vocalist can harmonize with existing parts or compose counterpoint and counter-rhythm BGV parts quite easily. Create a new track in Pro Tools for each BGV part to be added, then assign the vocal mic input to the new track and record the next part.

Another way to do this is by creating four new BGV tracks (or however many you will ultimately need). Record a new part on the first track, then drag the new audio clip into the next track. Repeat this until you have filled your BGV tracks.

Example: Enya is famous for stacking her vocals, in some cases more than 200 times in a song.

Group BGVs

This is a great way to build parts quickly and add new textures to your BGV sound. There are two ways to approach group vocals:

1. Use one or two small-diaphragm condenser microphones for the entire group. Adjust balance between singers by physically moving them closer to or further from the mics. This works really well for large groups or choirs recording in large rooms.
2. Give each singer his or her own microphone, and record each mic on its own track. This technique results in the most powerful BGV sound, but is only practical for small groups unless you have access to a large studio with quantities of headphones and microphones sufficient for the size of your group.

Stacking these group vocals can add even more power and depth to the BGV sound. I often use three singers in a group, stacked two or three times to make a huge vocal sound. In the mix, these parts can be panned hard left and hard right to dramatic effect.

To Tune or Not to Tune

There is a strange phenomenon in music right now, a sort of Jungian mass hysteria surrounding the insatiable desire for all music to be perfectly in tune and on the beat. Artists can and will decide exactly how in tune they wish to appear on a recording. There are a few different schools of thought on the subject, ranging from "just tune the occasional bit" all the way to "set it on stun and let it roll." If you listen to the Beatles, you will quickly realize they were singing amazingly in tune. In fact, if you listen to anything produced before the 1980s, the performances were natural and un-effected, because the technology to modify tuning simply did not exist. Now we have to consciously make the choice of whether to tune vocals or not. Usually it ends up being another quality threshold set by the production team. For example, if a note is more than 20 cents out, it gets tuned. The tools do exist, and they can be used tastefully or experimentally depending on where you establish that threshold of quality.

Auto-Tune vs. Melodyne vs. Waves Tune

There are a number tools used for tuning instruments or vocals, and while the results may be similar, the tools are applied differently.

Auto-Tune is a plug-in from Antares that is used to analyze and process single-note pitch correction in real-time. The technology allows you to establish parameters for processing, including key, scale selection, note inclusion/exclusion, sensitivity, and degree of effect. This processing is applied automatically in real-time. They have added a graphical editing mode that allows you to specify note correction on a per-note basis. This is a bridge to the other pitch-correction approach.

Melodyne is a product of the German company Celemony. Their approach is to first load the audio-to-be-tuned into their program, which is available as a stand-alone app with a plug-in bridge to port audio directly to and from the Pro Tools playlist, or a direct editing plug-in page. From there, you can graphically edit each note's pitch, duration, formant, amplitude, and pitch drift characteristics offline. Like the Antares plug-in, the processed audio is played back on the same Pro Tools track as the source, and can be written to disk with the real-time processing embedded. Melodyne recently announced their DNA (Direct Note Access) technology, which allows users to access and manipulate mono- and polyphonic content.

Waves Tune does basically what Melodyne does but with a plug-in editing page only, no stand-alone app.

There are other plug-ins available that do essentially the same job, but these are the main proponents of the technology.

Editing Your Recording

Editing = Making Choices

After recording a rock/pop/country record, you will likely have many more tracks than will actually make it to the final mix. There will come a time when you need to thin out parts that have been played throughout a song, editing them for content and to enhance the arrangement. You may ask yourself, "Do I really *need* to use all 14 of the guitar parts I recorded for this song?" A good rule of thumb is to listen to a rough mix of your song at a moderate to low volume. If you hear parts that conflict or compete for your attention, there's a good chance you may want to feature one part over another in the offending section. If a part cannot be heard among the mix, it may be due to a lack of level, or it may not fit in the song. Just because you recorded it does not mean it needs to be in the final mix! You do not have to use everything you record. Listen to some of the great hit songs, and you will hear sections where it might break down to just bass, drums, and vocal. This is the beauty of working in Pro Tools; you have the ability to test out arrangement ideas and save them as their own sessions for reference. You can easily create new song structures by moving sections around until you discover the perfect arrangement. You can just as easily undo edits to return to previous iterations in just a few seconds. Just remember: at some point you will actually have to make those choices and live with them.

Tracking a jazz group all at once might result in fewer edits than rock/pop/country, but you will have to make choices as to which solo to use, whether or not to edit a repetitive 64-bar intro, or just how loud the three cowbells want to be during the chorus. (Don't laugh, it's happened.)

The trick to all this is determining when the song is actually done. Theoretically, that should be the point at which the song assumes its best and highest form. Is it the first mix or the twelfth? Is it the third take? Was it better in the demo recording? These are subjective decisions at which you will arrive when you feel you have exhausted all possibilities of adding more tracks, more harmonies, and more hard drives. In contrast, consider the maestro Leonardo da Vinci, who is quoted as having said, "Art is never finished, only abandoned." Consider making some of these choices as you go along, rather than saving them all for the mix.

Recording Multiple Takes of a Song

If you spend enough time recording music, you may at some point experience the rare phenomenon of the "keeper first take." If this happens to you, make note of the details. This will likely become one of your better anecdotes.

More often than not, you will create a session for each song, record multiple takes of that song, then play these takes back for the band/artist to decide which version is the best. You will record each subsequent take after the previous take on the same timeline, so that you can see all takes in a linear and sequential order. Drop a marker at the beginning of each new take by typing the Enter key on the numeric keypad on your keyboard. You can name the marker "Take 1," for example, then add comments or information about that take in the Comments field. This is a good navigation tool to help audition takes, and a great way to keep track of the takes per song or per session. It's easy to create other location markers in this manner on the keeper take, so create song section markers (verse, chorus, bridge, solo, and so forth) when you hear a new section begin.

Editing Multiple Takes into a Master Take

It is common for a producer or artist to prefer different portions of different takes rather than one continuous take, and to ask the engineer to assemble these portions into a master take. This master take becomes the foundation for all future overdubs and edits on this song. This is often called "comping"; comp is short for *composite*, a technique with which you assemble selections from different takes into a single composite take.

The solution to this task is rather involved but quite manageable using standard Pro Tools editing functions. First, locate and mark the sections you wish to use from each take. For the sake of example, let's say that we will use:

- The *intro* section from take 1.
- The first *verse* from take 2.
- The first *chorus* from take 3.
- The *outro/ending* section of take 4. (Okay, so it's a short song.)

There are two ways to proceed from here: 1) when you have recorded with a click track, and 2) when you have not recorded with a click track.

If you recorded the song to a click track, enable Grid mode in bars/beats and resolve to one-bar increments.

Then:

- Create a new marker a minute or so beyond the end of the last take, and label it "Edited

Master Take." Make sure that your marker lies on the first beat of the nearest bar. This is where you will begin to assemble the new song.

- Turn on the All Groups function in the Groups window.
- Next, go to the intro section of the first take. Using the Cursor tool, drag a clip that encompasses the entire intro, from the first beat of the first bar to the first beat of the

bar following the intro. (Every track will be included if you enabled the All Groups function in the previous step.) Grid mode will ensure that your clip will conform exactly to the bar lines. Separate this clip by hitting the "B" key, Command + E, or by selecting from the main Edit menu: Edit > Separate Clip > On Grid. With this new clip selected, copy it by pressing the "C" key.

- Locate to the "Edited Master Take" marker and paste the intro by pressing the "V" key. The clip should appear beginning at the marker and extending to the end of the intro section. It should conform to the Bar/Beat grid as well.
- Next, go to the verse section of the second take. Using the Cursor tool, drag a clip that encompasses the entire verse, from the first beat of the first bar to the first beat of the bar following the verse. (Every track will be included if you enabled the All Groups function in the previous step.) Separate this clip by hitting the "B" key, Command + E, or by selecting from the main Edit menu: Edit > Separate Clip > On Grid. With this new clip selected, copy it by pressing the "C" key.
- Locate to the "Edited Master Take" marker and click in the timeline at the end of the intro you just pasted. Your cursor should be blinking there. Now, paste the verse by pressing the "V" key. The verse clip will appear right after the intro and should extend to the end of the verse section.
- Repeat this procedure for the remaining sections and any other sections you may wish to add.
- Voilà! You have just built the perfect take from the best parts of all the raw takes. If you did not record using a click track:
- As above, create a new marker a minute or so beyond the end of the last take, and label it "Edited Master Take." Make sure that your marker lies on or near the beginning of a full minute (e.g., 14:00.00). This is where you will begin to assemble the new song.
- Next, go to the intro section of the first take. We will learn to use a new tool to find the precise beginning of the first beat by using the Tab to Transients function to drive

the cursor to the beginning of the first audio transient. Click on the Tab to Transients button below the Tool Selector section at the top of the timeline in the Edit window. With this button enabled, you will be able to locate the next audio transient, as seen in the waveform display in the timeline.

- Click on a drum track, then hit the Tab key. The cursor should advance to a position just before the next audio transient.
- Drop a marker at this position labeled "Intro."
- Locate the end of the intro section, use the Tab to Transient function to locate the first beat of the next section, and drop a marker labeled "Verse."
- Turn on the All Groups function in the Groups window.
- Locate to the intro marker, then Shift + Click on the verse marker to select the entire intro clip. Separate the intro clip by hitting the "B" key or typing Command + E. With this new clip selected, copy it by pressing the "C" key.
- Locate to the "Edited Master Take" marker and paste the intro by pressing the "V" key. The clip should appear beginning at the marker and extending to the end of the intro section. While you're there, drop a new marker labeled "VERSE."
- Next, go to the verse section of the second take. Repeat the steps described in the intro step to isolate the entire first verse. Copy the verse section.
- Locate to the "VERSE" marker and paste the verse by pressing the "V" key. The verse clip will appear right after the intro and should extend to the end of the verse section.
- Repeat this procedure for the remaining sections and any other sections you may wish to add.
- Even without the grid, you have just built the perfect take from the best parts of all the raw takes.
- Now take a short break, you've earned it.

Note: You can disengage the All Groups function and fine-tune the transitions between sections track by track. You may need to adjust the clip borders one way or the other in order to accommodate slight timing differences between the end of one section and the beginning of another. Use your ears to determine if there are timing issues; use your eyes to identify where waveforms don't match up correctly.

Using Pro Tools Playlists

When you create a new track in a Pro Tools session, it is essentially an empty playlist waiting for you to record onto it or drag/import audio into it. Playlists can be managed by accessing the Playlist Selector, which enables you to create a new empty playlist, duplicate an existing playlist, delete a playlist, or select other existing playlists.

Using playlists to record a single (or multiple) track overdub gives you the ability to create alternate versions within an existing song in the timeline. Let's look at a practical example of how to use the Pro Tools playlist function.

Here's a common group tracking session occurrence: one musician performs his or her part correctly on an early take, while other musicians are still dialing in their parts. This can present a logistical challenge when the band wants to keep the drums from take 3, then overdub the remainder of the basic tracks on top of the take 3 drum track.

In this scenario, you would first duplicate the drum tracks playlist; next, create new playlists for the other instruments. This allows you to keep the drums intact on the timeline and add new parts from the other performers, who will be playing along with the drums and essentially overdubbing their parts. The complete original take will still exist in the playlist stack, so you can always go backward in time to that version if you need to.

If you engage the All Groups function, you can create or duplicate playlists globally merely by creating or duplicating a playlist on any track. This is another way to capture multiple takes, but in a vertical stack rather than in linear/sequential order.

Note: Anything you do to modify a duplicate playlist will be confined to that playlist. Edits, deletions, additions, and so forth will not affect the original playlist. Just remember to duplicate the playlist before editing. Take good notes in order to identify which playlist was the original version and avoid confusion.

Comping with Playlists

Previously we discussed comping takes in a linear session. Pro Tools has one of the slickest playlist comping interfaces of any DAW on the market. It's fast, easy, and great for the visually oriented engineer. Let's use a single-track overdub for this vocal comping example, and establish that the singer has performed the song from top to bottom four times on a track labeled "Vocal," with each pass on a new playlist. Our job is to assemble (or comp) a keeper vocal track from these four takes.

After each take, create a new playlist by clicking on the triangle icon next to the track name. Select "New…" and click to create a new empty playlist.

The default naming convention for a new or duplicated playlist is to retain the original playlist name and add ".01" as a suffix. Unless the name is otherwise modified, the suffix of each new playlist will increment. In this case, our four playlists will be labeled:

First pass:	*Vocal*
Second pass:	*Vocal.01*
Third pass:	*Vocal.02*
Fourth pass:	*Vocal.03*

In the Track View Selector, select Playlists.

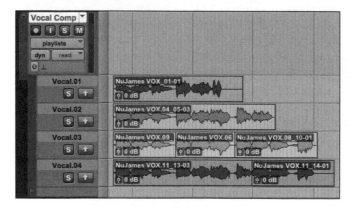

Assuming each vocal pass was recorded on a new playlist, there should now be four playlists visible.

Create a new playlist labeled "Vocal Comp." This new empty playlist should appear at the top of the playlist stack in the Vocal Track window.

Highlight and listen to phrases in sections of roughly 5 to 10 seconds in duration, beginning with the earliest pass (the "Vocal" playlist). If your transport is in Loop Play mode, you will be free to listen and switch between takes without having to constantly stop and start playback.

On the left side of the playlist lane, you will see the playlist name, a Solo button, and an Arrow button that performs the Copy Selection to Main Playlist function. Audition each phrase from within its playlist by clicking the Solo button to hear it in context with the rest of the mix.

Repeat this audition process for each playlist. When you have selected the best performance of the phrase, click the Copy Selection to Main Playlist button to promote that phrase to the main "Vocal Comp" playlist.

Do this one phrase at a time to assemble a seamless vocal comp track.

In the Track View Selector, select Waveform view to hide the playlists and return to the normal single-track view.

Recording Overdubs and Punch-ins

When adding new parts to existing tracks, prepare for the session by making sure that:
- Delay compensation is turned off, and you are using minimal plug-ins directly on tracks.
- QuickPunch mode is turned on.
- There is a countoff accessible and ready for the performer to hear.
- You have marked the sections of the song to make them easier to locate.

It's generally a good idea to use new playlists to record overdubbed performances; that way you can easily keep track of select tales and assemble them into a comp track. Use a duplicated playlist for punch-ins so that you can easily go back to the previous unaltered version of a performance if necessary.

Using QuickPunch, you can do single-track or multi-track punch-ins in Pro Tools; just make sure that *only* the desired tracks are record-enabled, otherwise you may end up unintentionally overwriting audio or MIDI information.

Tracking Tips

Document everything. Take notes on mic selection and placement, signal path, and outboard gear settings.

Document everything. Keep your notes on individual takes in case you need to find it later while editing.

Document everything. Keep everything. Record everything. Roll a 2-track backup of the entire live session to CDR or DAT if you can. The singer might hit that impossible lick in between takes…when the multi-track recorder is not rolling. You can always go back to the 2-track and edit it into the session after the fact.

Eric Schilling is a Grammy® and Emmy® award–winning engineer who records and mixes with Pro Tools HD using an AVID ICON control surface. When asked about tracking instruments, he talked about his method for recording multiple live performers and shared a clever organizational system he uses to record groups of instruments or vocals. On tracking, Eric says,

I am dogmatic about labeling everything in Pro Tools before I hit record. When I am actually recording live tracks with several musicians on the floor, I do not use multiple playlists but will record in linear order as I would on tape. This gives me a visual display of all my takes. I do use playlists when I get to individual players or vocalists.

For large tracking dates, I will build a template for that session with all track names, routing, record groups, etcetera, so as we move to record a new song, I can create a new session and import the tracks from the template, and I am all ready to go.

In typically modest fashion, he describes his system for recording a group of performers that require doubling passes.

I guess one small thing I do that may be a little different is the following: When recording strings, horns, background vocals, or anything else where you double and triple, I always prepare a Pro Tools session set up for that recording date. Let's use strings as an example. Say I am doing three passes of strings. I make a group for every pass that will enable record and lock volumes for all tracks.

In system prefs, I make sure the record button is not latching. So as I jump from

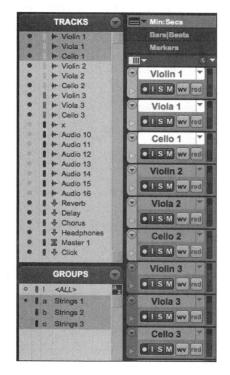

pass to pass, it will disarm the pass I have just completed when I arm the next.

Since tripling strings could take up 24 faders on a console, I route all passes out to the same faders (e.g., Violin L/R, Viola L/R, Cello L/R, Room L/R). In preferences, I make sure to uncheck the "Link Record and Play Faders" button.

With no string tracks armed, I set the volume of all string groups to -6 dB. As I arm each pass, I set the volume to 0 dB. So what happens? First, as I stack the strings, previous passes are played a little lower so I can feature the current pass I am recording. Second, this prevents buildup of volume as I stack passes.

At the end of your tracking day, back up everything on your hard drive to a second hard drive just to be safe. You never know what can happen to digital data overnight. In the dark. When no one is looking. Sometimes it just…goes away. Hard drives are cheap, so create a backup. Better safe than sorry.

Summary of Key Commands

Operation	Key Command
Plug-in Window Remains Open	Shift + Click Insert pane
Make Insert Inactive	Control + Command + Click Insert pane
Copy Plug-in Settings	Shift + Command + C
Paste Plug-in Settings	Shift + Command + V
Copy Plug-in	Option + Drag to new insert

Chapter 5 Review

1. Two of the most important choices a recording engineer must make involve mic _____ and _____.

2. True or False: The miking processes described in this chapter represent suggestions for a starting place only. _____

3. When recording an unfamiliar instrument, you should strive to make it sound like _____.

4. _____ requires rerecording a sound into your DAW using secondary processing.

5. True or False: Record-enabling a track in Pro Tools HD will bypass any native plug-ins inserted on that track. _____

6. The Record key commands are _____ + _____, _____, or _____ on the numeric keypad.

7. Excess headphone volume can alter your perception of _____.

8. Generally speaking, vocalists prefer to hear some _____ on their voice in the headphone mix.

9. _____ involves having a performer record his or her part again in perfect sync and tune with the original performance.

10. _____ or _____ can be an effective way to make background vocal tracks sound fuller.

11. _____ vocals with AutoTune or Melodyne has become a regular part of the music production process.

12. The process of assembling multiple takes into a single master take is known as _____.

13. To easily edit sections of music recorded to a click track, enable _____ mode resolved to bars/beats, then turn on the All _____ function. You will be able to edit and move sections of a song with greater rhythmic accuracy.

14. Pro Tools _____ function enables you to record multiple takes on a single track, then edit a keeper take without using additional tracks.

15. It's a good idea to record overdubs and punch-ins using _____ mode, so as not to risk missing a key portion of a performance by a late punch.

Chapter 6

SIGNAL PROCESSING TOOLS

In this section, we will look closely at ways to manipulate your tracks, whether recording with processing, bouncing processed audio clips to disk, or using real-time plug-ins.

Audio Suite Plug-ins

When used with clips selected in the sequence timeline, Audio Suite Plug-ins create (or *bounce*) new files with plug-in settings and add them to the clip list. These new files replace the original clips in your timeline. Audio Suite processing saves real-time processing power by permanently printing your effects.

Saving the session with the effects already printed gets you one step closer to having the session prepped for long-term archival or delivery.

Working with Plug-in Inserts

AAX: Avid Audio eXtension Plug-ins (Native)

- These plug-ins employ host-based processing to effect signal in real-time during playback.
- DigiRack Plug-ins are the 70-plus free plug-ins that ship with Pro Tools software. Check the AVID website for the latest list of plug-ins shipping with Pro Tools.
- Most of the virtual instruments used in Pro Tools and Pro Tools HD use AAX Native technology.
- Because Pro Tools is now a 64-bit application, its architecture is much more efficient. This means you can now access more virtual instrument plug-ins in real-time than you ever could before, as the application is no longer limited to just 2 GB of physical RAM.

AAX: Avid Audio eXtension Plug-ins (DSP)

- This type of plug-in requires the proprietary AVID PCIe cards, which use dedicated Digital Signal Processing (DSP) chips for real-time signal processing power, as opposed to using the host computer processing.
- The HDX system provides the power necessary to record/overdub/play back with minimal latency. (Not to be confused with ADC, which merely compensates for system latency on playback by making everything . . . later.)
- This is the most powerful type of Pro Tools system and requires a tower computer to accommodate the DSP cards.

  Note: You can only run AAX plug-ins on your system if you have the HDX processing cards. You can run AAX plug-ins on any system, but you need the HDX hardware to run both types.

Inserting Plug-ins

- Pro Tools gives you 10 plug-in inserts per track.
- You are limited only by your computer's processing power and RAM allocation.
- If you are working in the Edit window, click on the triangle icon in the Insert window. This will bring up an alphabetized list of all the plug-ins you have installed on your system. Mouse over a category—EQ, for example. The list will expand to show all available EQ plug-ins by name. Mouse over and select one of the EQ plug-ins and click. This will insert that plug-in on your track in the Insert slot you selected.

- To insert multiple plug-ins, select sequential slots and repeat the above procedure.
- The inserted plug-in will open in your main window as a floating pop-up window. You can position this window anywhere on your screen, preferably someplace where it won't interfere with the other windows. Clicking on the plug-in name will close the plug-in window.

- If you click on the name of another plug-in, the previous plug-in window will close, and the newly selected plug-in window will open.

Viewing Multiple Plug-in Windows

If the plug-in window is already open, click the red square target button to keep that particular window open. Then a new window will open for the next plug-in you select. You can leave any number of plug-in windows open while you work. Likewise, if you Shift + Click on the plug-in name in the Insert window, that plug-in will open and stay open until you close it manually.

Note: If you are working on a Pro Tools HDX system, Pro Tools software will now let you assign DSP or Native-based AAX plug-ins in any sequence, even alternating DSP/Native. You should be aware that inserting a native plug-in between DSP plug-ins will use additional voices. This will only be an issue if you are working on a massive mixing session with many tracks, and may result in track muting if you exceed the total number of available voices.

Plug-in Manipulation

Turning plug-ins on/off: some plug-ins use a proprietary on/off button, most simply use the Bypass button.

Bypass vs. Make Inactive:
- Bypass turns off the effect of the plug-in.
- It still uses system resources.
- Hint: Inactive plug-ins retain their settings but do not use system resources.
- To make an insert inactive, press Command + Control + Click on the Insert window.

Plug-ins use a series of mouse or control surface–adjustable controls to modify the various parameters displayed onscreen, which can be then be compared A/B style to default settings. Once you find a setting you like, the parameters can be saved for later recall by accessing the Plug-in Settings menu in the plug-in window. This menu allows you to copy, paste, save, and import settings, as well as setting the disk location for storing plug-in settings.

Copying Plug-in Settings

If you really dig the EQ sound you've got on your Left Overhead track and want to duplicate that on the Right Overhead track, you have a few options for matching settings.

- **Copy/Paste Settings:** In the plug-in window for the left overhead, locate the Preset menu, then select Copy Settings (Shift + Command + C). Insert the same plug-in on the Right Overhead track, locate the Preset menu, and select Paste Settings (Shift + Command + V).
- **Save the Setting:** If you found a sound you think you may use again and again, you can save it for easy future access. In the Left Overhead plug-in window, locate the

Preset menu, then select "Save Settings As…" This gives you the option to name the setting and save it among the other presets for future use.

- **Option + Drag:** This may be the quickest way to duplicate a plug-in; just copy the entire plug-in with settings intact to the destination insert (Option + Drag). Voilà!

The Secret of the Right Mouse-Click

The right mouse-click gives you access to hidden menu options depending on where you click. For example, right-click on the track name to show a menu of track options.

Right-click on a plug-in name in the Insert pane to show a menu of plug-in options:

This is a handy shortcut in case you forget the secret keystroke combination. If you have a one-button mouse, these menus are accessible by Control + Clicking.

Printing Tracks with Real-Time Plug-in Effects

If you're working on a project that you may need to revisit in the future, you should consider printing your edited tracks with effects.

Note: This is particularly valuable if there's chance that the project will be opened on a system without the same plug-ins or on a different DAW platform.

This process differs from printing files using Audio Suite plug-ins, in that the process is done in real-time using Aux tracks and internal bus routing. Here is a standard method for bouncing individual or group tracks:

Step 1: Create a new mono or stereo Aux Input track. Click on the Output pane of the source track Guitar and select "new track…" Name the Aux track some variation of the source name—e.g., "Guitar SUBMIX."

Step 2: Select the bus named "Guitar SUBMIX" for the output destination of the track(s) you wish to print with effects.

Step 3: Create a new mono or stereo Audio track (Shift + Command + N), and name it "Guitar Bounce."

Step 4: Select "Guitar SUBMIX" as the input for the "Guitar Bounce" track. Click the Record-Enable button, and record a clip from the beginning of the song. This new clip will be named "Guitar Bounce_01," and assuming you have engaged ADC, it will be perfectly in sync with the other tracks.

Step 5: Deactivate the original source tracks for this bounce so that they no longer play back or use system resources.

The newly created "Guitar Bounce" track now contains the guitar clips you bounced with effects and will be the track you use while mixing.

The process will be the same whether you bounce one track or several, as long as you remember to route all of the source tracks to the Aux Input you create. Side-Chain Effects

Here are some handy uses for side-chain effects.

- **Kick and Bass Compression:** This can be used to tighten up the low end of your mix by using a kick drum–keyed compressor side-chain input on your bass track to decrease the volume of the bass when the kick drum hits.
- **Kick Drum Augmentation Using an Oscillator:** Use the kick drum to key a noise gate open and closed on an oscillator track, generating a 20 Hz tone.
- **De-Essing:** Boosting a high frequency on an EQ inserted into a compressor plug-in uses the compressor to dynamically reduce the volume of that frequency range.
  Note that side-chain processing with native plug-ins uses additional voices.

Processing Tools for Your Toolkit

There are loads of tools available for you to create pristine, raw, or downright crushed and mutilated sounds. These tools generally fall into one of four categories:

- Frequency tools
- Dynamic Range Control tools
- Pitch tools
- Time-Based tools

Frequency Tools

EQ

EQ, or Equalization: Provides you with the means to increase or decrease the amplitude of a particular band of frequencies.

Parametric EQ: Gives you the ability to select a frequency center point, vary the bandwidth (or Q) of the effected frequencies, and make them louder or softer. Multi-band parametrics can be very powerful tools when combined to make notch filters.

Quasi-Parametric EQ: Pretty much like the parametric, but without the Q control. Used on many mid- and lower-priced mixing consoles.

Graphic EQ: Separates the frequency spectrum into fixed bands (typically 31), each with its own level control, which can then be made louder or softer independent of adjacent frequencies.

British-Style EQ: Made popular on British recording consoles, consisting of four equalization bands:

1. High shelf
2. Upper-mid parametric
3. Lower-mid parametric
4. Low shelf

EQs also include notch filters, bandpass filters, high-pass filters, and low-pass filters.

Pro Tools ships with three basic EQ plug-ins that are quite flexible, giving you the option of using a single band or up to seven bands of EQ that are user configurable. Think of the 7-band as a super-British EQ.

DigiRack EQ III plug-ins:

- 1-band equalizer, with six curve and filter profiles.
- 4-band equalizer, each band fully parametric. Low-frequency, low-mid, high-mid, high-frequency bands.
- 7-band equalizer, adds a mid-frequency band and two dedicated filters.

Using EQ to Fix Problems

You may encounter a problem that can only be fixed by applying the right EQ. For example, drums with an emphasized resonant frequency. Some snare drums can have a pronounced rise in mid-range frequency output, particularly around 1 kHz. Sometimes you can get rid of this ringing or resonance by tuning the drum slightly lower or by physically damping one of the heads of the drum. Back in the day, drummers used to put their fat wallets on the drumhead to deaden the ring. If your drummer doesn't have a particularly fat wallet, or if you like the tone of an unrestricted snare drum, you may want to consider EQing some of that midrange information out of the snare-drum mic channel before recording.

Suggestion: Sweep a peak EQ across the spectrum at +6 dB to isolate the offending frequency. Once located, change the amplitude setting to -6 dB and see if that is sufficient to reduce the problem. Adjust amplitude and frequency to fine-tune the fix.

Just remember: Anything you do in the recording process cannot be undone in the mix, so be sure to make your EQ choices carefully. If you're unsure, leave it *flat* (un-EQed).

Using EQ to Enhance Sound

EQ can be used to emphasize frequencies that are not sufficiently present in a recording, such as the high end of cymbals or the low end of a kick drum.

There are two ways to apply EQ:

Subtractive EQ: Making a selected frequency or frequencies quieter.

For example, kick drum: Subtracting -3 dB @ 400 Hz, medium Q, with a parametric equalizer can make a kick drum fit better with a bass or guitar track.

Additive EQ: Making a selected frequency (or frequencies) louder.

For example, electric guitar: Adding +3dB @ 3kHz with a peak EQ can make an electric guitar sound more prominent in a mix.

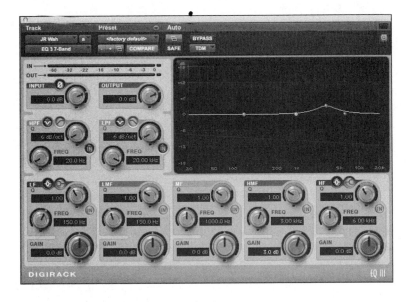

Try making subtractive changes before you start adding gain to your EQ. Folks generally tend to reach for additive EQ right away—I strongly suggest you determine what your objective is first, then see which frequencies you can reduce in order to achieve the objective. (See the kick drum/bass guitar example.)

Note: A well-recorded instrument may sound great alone but might not work with other instruments in a mix. For example, an acoustic guitar recording might sound full and have a wide frequency response but compete with other instruments in a mix. It may be necessary to thin out some of the low-end information in the acoustic guitar track by reducing the low-frequency shelf EQ by -3 dB at 150 Hz. The resulting sound may not be the perfect solo acoustic guitar sound, but it will work better in context with other chordal instruments.

Dynamic Range Control

Compression/Limiting

The compressor is perhaps the most misunderstood piece of gear in the studio, largely because it's difficult for the untrained ear to hear exactly what a compressor does. A good compressor well used may not even be discernible in a track. Here's a simple guide to comp/limiters...

A compressor or limiter is used to control the dynamic range of a performance. The difference between a compressor and a limiter is the gain reduction ratio, as in:

< 10:1 = compression

> 10:1 = limiting

What does the ratio relate to? Input to output gain comparison. Look at it this way: assuming your ratio is set at 2:1, if your input signal increases 2 dB above the threshold, your output level will only increase by 1 dB.

At 4:1, for every increase of 4 dB above the input threshold, the output will increase 1 dB.

At 20:1, for every increase of 20 dB on the input, the output will increase 1 dB.

At a ratio of infinity:1...well, you can do the math.

There are two kinds of compressors, in my opinion. There are units that are clean, clinical, and fairly transparent sonically, and units that are dirty and distorted and sound amazing if used/abused in the right manner. And of course, there are a few that can do both depending on how you set them up.

While I don't generally believe in "one size fits all" solutions for equipment settings, there is a basic compressor setting that will get you started with just about any recording. This setting gives you clean dynamic range control without being terribly obvious. It looks like this: 2:1 ratio, 10 ms attack, 150 ms decay, set threshold for no more than -6 dB gain reduction. Use it on a vocal track to get it to sit properly in a mix, use it on room mics to get a drum set to sound more aggressive, use it on just about any track to even out dynamics for mixing. Obviously, this won't work in every situation; you wouldn't use this setting on a stereo mix bus, for example.

You may find it useful to insert an external hardware compressor in circuit after the mic pre-amp when recording tracks. Another common solution is to use a mic pre/compressor channel strip to add compression before the signal is recorded.

You can use plug-ins to process tracks being recorded; however, you will need to set up a send/return chain using an Aux bus and record the output of the processed Aux return. Keep in mind, this will introduce some delay, and the compression cannot be undone.

Pro Tools comes with a DigiRack Compressor/Limiter: Dynamics III.

Multi-Band Compression

Multi-band compressors are an amalgam of a crossover, an EQ, and a compressor. This handy device allows you to select a frequency band or bands to compress independently of its neighboring frequencies. Used most often in mastering, it can also be used to add polish to a vocal track, drum track, or anything with complex frequency content that needs to be managed.

One of the great features of multi-band compression is the ability to use different dynamic control settings on each band. You could use a quick-attack, quick-release setting with GR of -6 dB on the low-frequency band; a fast-attack, slow-release setting with GR of -1.5 dB on the mid-range band; and a slow-attack, slow-release setting with -3dB GR on the high band. By contrast, a single-band compressor uses one ratio, one attack time, one release time, and one threshold to process all frequencies that pass through the device.

Pro Tools does not include a multi-band compressor in the standard complement of plug-ins. There are a number of great third-party units out there; my personal preference is for the iZotope Ozone 5 (AAX Native) or the WAVES C6 (AAX/Native).

Expanders/Noise Gates

An expander (or downward expansion circuit) is a gentler form of noise gate and is the functional opposite of a compressor. An expander reduces the level of a signal below a threshold, whereas the compressor decreases the level of signal above a threshold.

An expansion ratio of 2:1 will result in a level reduction of 2 dB for every 1 dB below threshold. So a signal drop of 2 dB below threshold would result in a further reduction of 4 dB.

At a 4:1 ratio, the output level would drop -4 dB for every -1 dB below threshold. Hence, a -2 dB drop would result in level reduction of -8 dB on output.

At ratios of 10:1 or higher, the expander becomes a noise gate.

Noise gates are used frequently in live sound production but can also be used effectively in an environment that is inherently noisy. High-gain guitar amplifiers are particularly noisy and can benefit from gentle application of a noise gate. Most often noise gates are used in mixes, but under extraordinary circumstances, they can be useful in recording tracks.

Pro Tools comes with an Expander/Gate that has an optional Look Ahead feature, the purpose of which is not actually to see into the future but rather to assess the attack time required to preserve transients and delay the output by that amount.

De-Essers

A de-esser can be used to dynamically control the high-frequency saturation on a vocal when *s*'s and *t*'s are emphatically and vigorously uttered. There are hardware and software de-essers which can be used in tracking or mixing.

In the absence of a hardware or plug-in de-esser, you can construct one using your EQ III plug-in and Dynamics III plug-in. Place the EQ first in the chain followed by the compressor. Adjust the high-frequency shelf (or notch) to emphasize the problem frequency. (I know, sounds counterintuitive, but hang in there for a minute.) Then use the EQ plug-in to trigger the key input on the compressor. Varying the EQ frequency and amplitude boost, as well as the amount of gain reduction on the compressor, will yield a surprisingly effective method of controlling sibilance in a vocal track. Just don't overdo it.

Pro Tools comes with a dedicated de-esser plug-in as part of the DigiRack series. Insert this plug-in before you compress or EQ your vocal tracks, or your processing might make the job of de-essing much less effective.

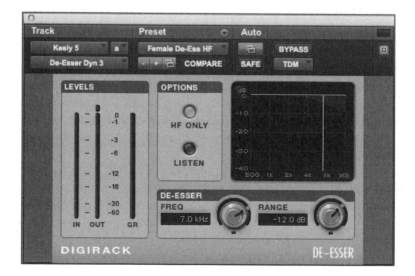

Pitch Tools

Pitch Change

A pitch-change plug-in can be automated to create a dynamic change in a performance. If a sax part has one note that is consistently out of tune, a pitch plug-in can be set to correct the intonation for each occurrence. The AAX DigiRack plug-in, Pitch II, allows you to raise or lower pitch up to an octave, and works in real-time. This function is automatable.

Note: If you want to make the pitch change more permanent, these effects can also be applied using Audio Suite Pitch Shift processing to create new pitch-altered clips, thereby keeping the real-time host processing demands to a minimum. This can be time consuming, which brings us to the alternative...

Auto-Pitch Correction

Auto-pitch correction tools have gotten very sophisticated, and can take the automation task out of the hands of the engineer and place it in the realm of the computer and its ability to make lightning-fast calculations to analyze changes in pitch. Using a frequency-counter function to determine the half-wave pitch of the note as performed, the plug-in determines the nearest note played, then calculates the pitch change necessary to bring that note into tune. This is a real-time operation and uses a great deal of processing power to accomplish. Examples of auto-tuning plug-ins would be Antares Auto-Tune, Melodyne, and WavesTune.

Creative Use of Pitch Effects

Caution: Use subtly and sparingly. Overuse can cause nausea or motion sickness.

- **Chorus:** To make a chorus effect, take a stereo pitch-change plug-in and set the left-side pitch at +6 cents and the right side at -6 cents. Adjust the mix control to determine the amount of chorus effect. (Reference the Mike Stern School of Clean Guitar Tone.)
- **Harmonies:** Using a mono pitch-change plug-in to add a higher octave to a bass guitar: Set mix control at 50 percent. This effect is particularly effective when used in a trio setting or sparsely orchestrated song. Try tuning it an octave below when used with a lead guitar part. (Think Prince.) You can set it to other intervals as well for chord or harmony effects.

Time-Based Effects

Phase-Reverse

Phase errors can occur when there are minute timing differences between two or more microphones capturing the same sound source. Phase errors are the bane of multi-track recording. A phase-reverse plug-in (or activating the phase flip on an EQ or other plug-in) will shift the phase of that signal by 180 degrees, thereby reversing the phase error and eliminating a great deal of unwanted cancellation—or reinforcement—of frequencies when mixing.

To check phase on two tracks: Pan them mono, adjust levels equally. Then reverse the phase on one track. You may have a phase problem if:

- The signal drops in level.
- The signal increases in level.
- A portion of the frequency spectrum gets quieter.
- A portion of the frequency spectrum gets louder.

- The signal goes away completely.

If you encounter any of these problems, you are hearing phase cancellation in the recording. Use the phase-reversal function on a short-delay (or other) plug-in to determine the setting that most faithfully represents the sound of the original recorded instrument.

Phase is particularly hard to control when recording/mixing a drum kit. Good miking practice when recording is just about the only solution to this problem.

Prevention is the best cure, so remember the 3 to 1 rule when recording. (Two microphones must be three times farther from each other than the distance to the sound source when recording.)

Most of the DigiRack EQ and dynamics plug-ins incorporate a phase reverse button into their designs.

Reverb

Reverb is the third temporal stage of sound in an acoustic space, after direct sound and early reflection. Reverb is a complex series of delays that appear to be indistinct to our ears, and give space and depth to sound. Think about the sound you hear after bouncing a basketball in a gymnasium. Big halls with long reverb decay times (>3 seconds) are good for slow songs, vocals, sparse arrangements, or special effects. Rooms with medium decay times (1–3 seconds) are good for general use with all instruments. Plates or small rooms with short decay times (<1.5 seconds) are good for percussive sounds and up-tempo songs.

Don't forget that bastion of the '80s pop music, the nonlinear reverb, a.k.a., "the Phil Collins drum sound." Phil didn't invent it, but he sure did popularize it. It's still a valid tool, especially when trying to make a snare drum sound bigger in the mix. Just don't overdo it.

Reverbs are usually applied as parallel processing in a send/return configuration using aux tracks. You can use a dedicated reverb plug-in per track, but it will consume lots of CPU cycles by the time you instantiate a reverb plug-in on every track that requires 'verb. It's also easier to change settings on one or two plugs rather than duplicating settings across multiple instances of a reverb plug-in.

Pro Tools ships with a number of reverb plug-ins, including AIR Nonlinear Reverb, AIR Reverb, AIR Spring Reverb, and D-Verb.

Delay

Delay is a repeated sound, which can be heard as a discrete audio event occurring a short interval of time after the original event. It can be a single echo or multiple repeats.

- Short delays (< 100 ms) create a doubling effect.
- Medium delays (100–200 ms) are used for slapback delay and tape delay emulation. Think rockabilly music or some of the classic Sun Records recordings of Elvis, Johnny Cash, Carl Perkins, and so on.
- Long delays (> 200 ms) appear as discrete echoes of the original sound and can be used to lengthen the apparent duration of a sound or performance.
- Pro Tools delay plug-ins give you the option of setting delay times based on tempo and note durations, making it much easier to create musical delay settings without reaching for your calculator.
- Pro Tools comes with the following delay plug-ins: AIR Dynamic Delay, AIR Multi Delay, and Mod Delay III

Modulation Effects

These are also time-based effects, but the pitch can be dynamically altered by an LFO to produce sweeping effects, such as flanging or chorus.

- Flanging occurs between 2 and 10 ms.
- Chorus effects occur between 10 and 50 ms.
- Pro Tools ships with the following modulation effect plug-ins: AIR Chorus, AIR Ensemble, AIR Flanger, AIR Multi Chorus, AIR Phaser, and Sci-Fi.

Time Compression/Expansion, or TCE

Used for lengthening or shortening the duration of a file or clip. Can be applied as an Audio Suite process or as an editing function when the Time Compression/Expansion mode is selected for the Trimmer tool.

For obvious reasons, a new file is written when this effect is applied. It gets back to that "no seeing into the future" thing we covered earlier.

Other Effects

Distortion

In the world of audio, distortion occurs when signal processing changes the basic shape of an audio waveform. An example would be the overmodulated clipping of a sine wave resulting in a square wave—a distortion of the original waveform.

Remember when I wrote about learning the rules so you could break them later? Okay, now's your big chance. We usually avoid all types of distortion when recording tracks, but yes, you can use distortion as an intentional effect in the recording process. It serves multiple duties, because distortion can add harmonic richness, distinctive equalization, and dramatic compression effects, all using one plug-in properly applied. Pro Tools comes with a brilliant guitar amp emulator, called, simply, Eleven. (Google *This Is Spinal Tap* for the original reference.) It sounds killer on guitar of course, but it can also lend a dramatic sense of urgency to a variety of other instruments and vocals.

There are two ways to use distortion effects in your mix:

Option 1: Apply the Eleven plug-in as an insert on an Aux Input, then use Aux sends from individual channels to send audio to the plug-in in parallel to the normal output. This allows you to dynamically mix the effect to taste in the context of your mix. The send can also be easily automated.

Option 2: Apply the Eleven plug-in directly onto a track insert, and tweak until you achieve the perfect amount of distortion for your track. The plug-in parameters can still be automated, but you will not be able to control the balance of un-effected track to effected track quite so easily. This method is good if you want the effect during the entire song and don't need to obsess over the subtleties.

You can try to introduce distortion by overdriving one of your EQ or dynamics plug-ins, but do so cautiously, or it may result in harsh digital clipping. (This is a whole other sonic animal than the pleasing low-order harmonic enhancing effects of a nice tube amp or distortion pedal.) Distortion can be very effective on drum sub-mixes as an enhancement. See Nine Inch Nails for reference examples. Joe Barresi is one of a handful of producers who effectively use distortion as a creative tool on instruments other than just guitar.

Panning

Pan is the term used to describe the distribution of signal in the panorama between the left and right channels or speakers. In strategizing your recording project beforehand, you probably thought about how to present the instruments across the pan spectrum. The most common practice in panning is to present the song in the stereo field as it might be heard in a live performance, with instruments panned roughly as they might appear on stage. There are plenty of opportunities to get creative with panning, including automating pan sweeps to tempo or using delays to alternate side to side.

Don't be afraid to use the entire stereo field. You can pan things to the extremes and still be subtle, musical. Season to taste and find the right effect for the song.

Other Tools and Plug-ins

Pro Tools comes with more than 70 useful and creative plug-ins, which should provide you with hours of entertainment. I have already described a number of the more common plug-ins. The remaining plugs range from metering devices to guitar amp emulators and virtual instruments. You will also find lo-fi plug-ins for sound design applications or creative applications of audio distortion.

Elastic Audio

AVID has found a way to see into the future just enough to change the tempo of a recorded track without altering the pitch. And yes, it happens in real-time.

Elastic Audio changes tempos in real-time by using time compression/expansion (TCE) to achieve dynamic tempo changes. This operation is tied to the tempo of the track and will vary the tempo of a recorded performance based on the sequence tempo.

Beat Detective

Beat Detective was originally designed as an automated module to help edit and change the timing of drum parts. Before Beat Detective, this type of editing was done manually and was a slow and painstaking operation. Now it's easy to fix timing on sections of multiple tracks, change tempos, and change or apply groove characteristics to a live performance using this handy—but fairly complex—module.

The difference between Beat Detective and Elastic Audio is that Elastic Audio uses TCE to alter clip length to make timing and tempo changes, whereas Beat Detective edits a track or tracks into tempo-delineated sub-clips and shifts the timing of those clips in relation to one another according to the current tempo and grid settings, but without altering clip length.

We will examine Beat Detective and Elastic Audio in greater detail later in this series of books.

Summary of Key Commands

Operation	Key Command
Solo Safe	Command + Click Solo button
Split Clip	B, or Command + E

Chapter 6 Review

1. _____ plug-ins process audio and create new audio clips, saving the CPU power it takes to process effects in real-time.
2. AAX is an acronym for _____ plug-ins, which refers to the propriety plug-in format for Pro Tools.
3. Pro Tools ships with more than _____ AAX plug-ins included.
4. In order to use HDX hardware, you must have an _____ authorization for Pro Tools HD and one or more _____ cards installed in your computer.
5. Pro Tools gives you up to _____ inserts per track for plug-ins.
6. The three ways to disable a plug-in are via an _____ button, _____ button, or by making the insert _____.
7. In order to save system resources and free up voices, you may have to make plug-ins inactive by _____ + _____ + _____ on the insert button associated with the plug-in you wish to deactivate.
8. Plug-in settings can be saved using the _____ menu in the plug-in window.
9. The easiest way to copy a plug-in from one insert to another is to _____ + _____ the source insert to the destination insert slot.
10. The right-mouse click is a timesaver, providing extra menus accessible by clicking around in the Edit and Mix windows. How do you access the right-click menu with a one-button mouse? _____ + _____
11. You can print tracks with effects using two methods. The first by using _____ plug-ins, and the second by recording effected clips to another track using an _____ Input for routing.
12. Audio processing tools fall into one of the following categories:
    a. _____
    b. _____
    c. _____
    d. _____
13. You can add or subtract the amplitude of selected frequency bands using an _____.
14. A dynamic range control ratio of 8:1 indicates compression, while a ratio of 20:1 indicates _____.
15. An expander becomes a _____ at ratios greater than 10:1.
16. A multi-band compressor is a combination of crossover, an EQ, and a compressor, and allows you to selectively compress _____.
17. The function of a de-esser is to reduce the _____ in a vocal performance.
18. _____ cancelation can occur when two or more microphones pick up the same sound source.
19. Modulation effects, such as chorus and flanging, are _____ effects.
20. Reverb is actually a complex series of _____, which our ears hear as diffuse space.
21. To correct the pitch, or tuning, of a recorded performance, you can use a manual _____ plug-in for single notes, or an _____ tool such as Antares Auto Tune or Melodyne.
22. Panning is an important tool to distribute energy across the _____ field.
23. _____ is the alteration of an audio waveform. This can result in an unpleasant sound or be used as a powerful creative tool.
24. _____ and _____ are Pro Tools functions that can be used to adjust the timing of recorded audio performances.

Chapter 7
CLOSING THOUGHTS

Know Your Tools

If you take the time to develop a deep understanding of the capabilities of Pro Tools, you will be able to work faster, more efficiently, and more accurately. This is important, because inspiration waits for no one. If you get an idea, you should be able to act on it immediately without having to search the manual or call a tech just to figure out how to implement your idea.

Record Clean Tracks

I learned to record in an environment that prized clean and pristine recording of basic tracks. While you can always add distortion or other effects to the audio in your mix, you cannot take those things away if they are recorded on the track. There is no perfect un-reverb or de-compression plug-in, insofar as I am aware. Make sure there are no buzzes or other noises you'll have to deal with later.

Experiment

Pro Tools gives you lots of options for playing around with edits and recording techniques; don't be afraid to try new things. Make note of the things that work, and remember the things that do not.

Back Up Your Work!

This cannot be stressed enough. Keep a hard drive backup of everything you do; make two backups on different formats if you can.

Have an Opinion

Don't be afraid to offer creative input when working with an artist. Be reasonable, of course, but many performers are looking for an objective and unbiased opinion on a part, a sound, or a performance. Be direct, but remember to be *kind*. Put yourself in the shoes of the performer, and speak to him or her as you would have someone speak to you when you are baring your innermost creative soul.

R.E.S.P.E.C.T.

Be respectful of the opinions of the artist. It may be difficult to understand the motivation behind certain parts or sounds, lyrics or vocalizations. Take the time to find out as much as you can about the meaning of the song before offering the aforementioned creative input.

Rapport

Develop a rapport with the artist. This may be the most important advice I can offer you. If an artist or performer is comfortable with you and feels like he or she can communicate well with you, there is an excellent chance that you can coax extraordinary performances from him or her. There is no known plug-in to emulate trust.

Have Fun!

Don't forget, we get to make music, and music is fun. Every day you get to record or make music is a good day. May all your days be good!

GLOSSARY

Here are some commonly used audio terms or abbreviations that will clarify portions of this book:

Auth. An abbreviation for **authorization**.

bad. A negative subjective opinion held by this author. Synonyms include *inconsistent*, *less-than-stellar*, and *poor*. There is no consistently measurable threshold beneath which something is bad. Use your best judgment.

channel. An audio path; may be mono or multiple channels. Customarily associated with recording consoles and tape recorders, *channel* can also be used to describe the audio signal path into and out of a DAW. MIDI *channels* are independent data streams that can be routed to specific input and output devices, both internal and external to the DAW.

comp. An abbreviation for **composite**. To combine/compile the best parts of multiple takes into a single master take, as in *comping* a vocal track.

DAW. An abbreviation for **Digital Audio Workstation**.

dB (FS). An abbreviation for **Decibels Full Scale**. 0 dB(FS) is equivalent to maximum amplitude at the threshold of clipping, 100 percent modulation of digital signal, or no more headroom.

dBVU. An abbreviation for **Decibel Volume Units**. Used for measuring average audio signal amplitude. 0 dBVU is equivalent to about -14 dB(FS). 0 dBVU is standard reference for +4 dBVU balanced audio systems and equates to AC current of 1.23 volts (for the tech geeks out there).

decibel. One-tenth of a *bel* (which is seldom used in measurement). Though *dB* can reference a number of measurements, we will be primarily be using *dB (SPL)* to measure loudness in the studio, and dB (FS) to reference headroom and maximum signal level. Also **dB**.

DI. An abbreviation for **Direct Injection, Direct Input**, or **Direct Interface**. An electronic audio device used to match impedance and level, usually between musical instruments and recording devices or PA systems. Can be active or passive. Also called **DI Box**.

good. A positive subjective opinion often promoted by this author. Equivalent terms include *great*, *brilliant*, *killer*, and *awesome*. There is no known scientific method for measuring *good*; use your own criteria.

GTR. An abbreviation for **guitar**.

menu. A list of functional options that can be accessed from the top of the Main Edit window or within other pop-up windows.

pane. A smaller component within a window, typically providing access to a specific set of parameters or options. This book refers to Insert *panes*, Send *panes*, Track *panes*, and other such "sub-windows."

pass. Common usage: "Give me another *pass* at that guitar solo." See also **take**.

peak meter. Designed to respond accurately to very fast audio transients, such as drum hits. This is the type of meter emulated in Pro Tools displays.

PNO. An abbreviation for *piano*.

PPM. An abbreviation for *Peak Program Meter*. See also *peak meter*.

SPL. An abbreviation for *Sound Pressure Level*, as measured in *dB (SPL)*.

take. Refers to a recorded performance, as in a vocal *take*. See also *pass*.

TCE. An abbreviation for *Time Compression and/or Expansion*.

track. (noun) Depending on the context, this can refer to a recorded song or a recorded performance, and in Pro Tools, refers to a session playlist created to record or play back audio, video, or MIDI information.

track. (verb) The act of performing or recording a song or parts of a song—e.g., when recording a jazz piece, one usually *tracks* all of the musicians at once.

VU meter. Typical use of an analog *VU meter* is to measure the average amplitude of an audio signal over time. Hence, the rise time and fall time of a *VU meter* are each about 300 milliseconds. Not good for reading peak program amplitude.

window. A portion of the onscreen display, which provides visual display and access to a set of Pro Tools functions. Examples are the Edit window, the Mix window, the Transport window, and so on.

APPENDIX: ONLINE VIDEO TUTORIALS AND PRO TOOLS SESSIONS

Video Content

The accompanying video tutorials demonstrate the concepts and techniques explained in *Producing Music with Pro Tools 11*. The featured sessions were recorded in an earlier version of Pro Tools that used the term "region" when referring to sections of audio and MIDI data on the timeline and tracks of the edit and arrange windows. Pro Tools 11 now calls these audio and MIDI sections "clips."

Videos 1–3 introduce you to the world of Pro Tools.

Videos 4–6 discuss screen layout, basic operation, and editing functions.

Videos 7–12 show how to effectively configure your virtual studio in order to record basic tracks, record overdubs, and prepare your session for mixing.

Video 13 summarizes the recording process.

1. Introduction

Welcome to the world of *Recording Instruments and Vocals in Pro Tools*.

2. Launching Pro Tools

Understanding how to open existing sessions or create new ones is the first step in Pro Tools proficiency. This segment shows:

- The proper order for powering up your Pro Tools system
- Where to store audio and session files
- How to efficiently manage the DAW from the first mouse click

3. How to Use the Session Files

Downloading the tutorial material to your hard drive, opening sessions, and keeping track of data is important to your learning experience and to your workflow. This tutorial helps ensure that you don't lose your assets!

4. Edit/Mix Window Layout

Getting around in Pro Tools is easier when you understand the window layout. This tutorial will guide you through the:

- Edit window
- Mix window
- Top menu bar
- Edit modes

5. Transport Functions

Pro Tools navigation is simple and elegant, yet has many configuration options for customizing the creative work environment. This segment focuses on:

- Counters and status displays
- Record options

- Playback options
- Creating and managing markers
- Creating custom Window Configurations

6. Data Management

This tutorial digs deep into the best ways to get data in and out of Pro Tools. It demonstrates methods to easily create and locate templates, session file versions, and more. Overviews of these important functions are included:

- Import audio
- Import session data
- Export as AAF/OMF
- Bounce to disk

7. Building a Virtual Studio

Pro Tools lets the user configure a mixer so that it provides exactly what's needed to record each song. Explore the various tools available to design the ideal virtual console and see how to use that design as a starting place for future sessions.

8. Using Direct Plug-ins

Plug-ins are fundamental creative building blocks in the development of virtually every mix. This video demonstrates the use of plug-ins, inserted directly on a recorded track, to control dynamics, adjust EQ, and control pitch.

It also shows the differences between—and recommends some uses for—serial and parallel processing. This segment helps you avoid some of the biggest (and most common) processing mistakes made by beginning DAW users.

9. Using Auxiliary Inputs

Whether adding reverb to tracks or creating a headphone mix, the auxiliary input is a very powerful weapon in the recording arsenal. Learn to maximize flexibility and minimize system resources using aux buses.

10. Recording and Playback

Pro Tools can be operated as a simple recording device or a nimble and highly configurable DAW. Learning the array of recording and playback commands will let you configure transport capabilities to match your workflow. In this video, we will cover use of the following:

- Transport Window Options
- Record Options
- Playback Options
- Loop Recording with Playlists

11. Pro Tools Playlists

Tracking with playlists can make it easy to work with scratch tracks, click tracks, or alternate versions. In this segment, we will examine how to use playlists when editing basic tracks, overdubbing instruments, and comping vocal takes.

12. Setting Up a Rough Mix

At some point in the recording process, you will need to create a reference mix, or rough mix, for yourself or others to evaluate. This segment will show you how to quickly set up a basic rough mix, add effects, and bounce the mix to disk.

13. In Conclusion

This video segment contains final comments from the author.

Audio Content

The three Pro Tools sessions used in these video exercises are included online. They provide an opportunity to get some hands-on experience using professionally recorded multi-track masters! Use them to explore the vast array of tools and techniques available to Pro Tools power users.

ANSWER KEY FOR CHAPTER REVIEW QUESTIONS

Chapter 1
1. Pro Tools 11, 64
2. delay, I/O
3. iLok
4. delay, HDX
5. DSP, PCI-e, HDX DSP
6. usage, processing
7. AAE or system
8. Higher, AAX
9. N, I/O
10. internal, external
11. ADAT, S/PDIF
12. I/O settings
13. Shuffle, Slip, Spot, Grid
14. Zoomer, Trim, Selector, Grabber, Scrubber, Pencil
15. Smart
16. mouse click, keyboard

Chapter 2
1. -2.5dB, -3dB, -4.5dB, and -6dB
2. output, routing
3. pre, post-fader
4. hardware inserts, interface, external
5. voices, latency
6. reverb, sends
7. Command + Drag
8. delay or latency, hardware
9. 10, 10
10. Master fader
11. Option + C
12. group, command
13. tempo
14. transport
15. edit, mix
16. m , . /
17. enter, 999
18. Command + S
19. Strip Silence
20. consolidate

Chapter 3

1. d. All of the above
2. True
3. AIFF, WAV
4. Spacebar, 0
5. 5
6. Wait for Note, Metronome, Conductor
7. Time Code
8. True (Pro Tools 9), False (Pro Tools 10 and higher)
9. Shift + Spacebar
10. Control + click
11. a. Normal
    b. Record
    c. Loop Record
    d. Destructive Record
    e. QuickPunch
    f. playlist
    g. QuickPunch
12. playlist
13. QuickPunch
14. Track, Click
15. peak level
16. headroom
17. headphone mix system
18. pan
19. HD Omni
20. Save As

Chapter 4

1. tracking
2. transducer
3. phantom power
4. False (unless you are using a Royer R122!)
5. Direct Input, Direct Injection
6. microphone pre-amplifier
7. compressor
8. frequency
9. parametric
10. Digital Audio Workstation
11. audio interface, or I/O
12. near-field, mid-field
13. False
14. signal chain
15. latency
16. Automatic Delay Compensation

Chapter 5

1. selection, placement
2. True
3. it sounds in the room
4. re-amping
5. True
6. Command + Spacebar, F12, 3
7. pitch
8. reverb
9. doubling
10. Automatic Double Tracking, ADT
11. Tuning
12. comping
13. Grid, groups
14. playlist
15. QuickPunch

Chapter 6

1. Audio Suite
2. Avid Audio eXtension
3. 70
4. iLok, HDX
5. 10
6. on/off, bypass, inactive
7. Command, Control, clicking
8. Preset
9. Command, drag
10. Control + click
11. Audio Suite, Auxiliary
12. frequency, dynamic range, pitch tools, time-based effects
13. equalizer, or EQ
14. limiting
15. noise gate
16. frequency bands
17. sibilance
18. phase
19. time-based
20. delays
21. pitch change, auto-pitch correction
22. stereo
23. distortion
24. Elastic Audio, Beat Detective

INDEX